# Mesa and Tex-Mex

## A Southwest Cookbook Featuring Authentic Mesa Recipes and Tex-Mex Recipes

By
BookSumo Press

Published by
http://www.booksumo.com

# LEGAL NOTES

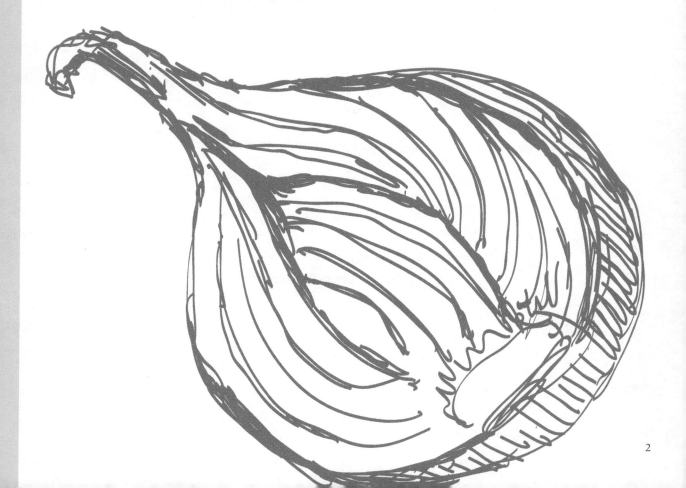

# Table of Contents

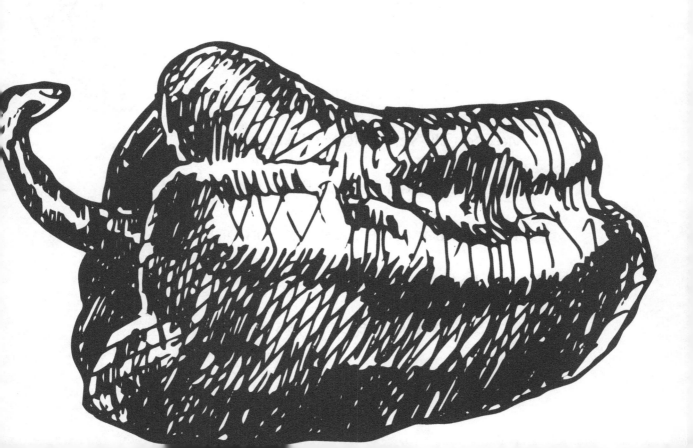

# Mesa
# Apple Salad

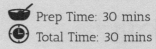 Prep Time: 30 mins

Total Time: 30 mins

| Servings per Recipe: 12 | |
| --- | --- |
| Calories | 272 kcal |
| Fat | 19.5 g |
| Carbohydrates | 24.4g |
| Protein | 3.7 g |
| Cholesterol | 7 mg |
| Sodium | 165 mg |

## Ingredients

Dressing:
2/3 C. light olive oil
1/2 C. white sugar
1/3 C. freshly squeezed orange juice
1 tbsp poppy seeds
2 tsp minced onion
1 tsp Dijon mustard
1 tsp grated orange zest
1/2 tsp salt
Salad:
1 (5 oz.) package spring mix salad greens

1 bunch green onions, chopped
1 avocado, chopped
1 green apple, cored and chopped
1 pkg. (4 serving size) crumbled goat cheese
1/2 C. sweetened dried cranberries
1/2 C. golden raisins
1 (3 oz.) can mandarin oranges, drained
1/4 C. seasoned walnuts

## Directions

1. For the dressing in a blender, add all the ingredients and pulse till smooth.

2. In a large salad bowl, mix together all the salad ingredients.

3. Place the dressing and toss to coat well.

# TUCSON
# Chili

Prep Time: 20 mins
Total Time: 12 hr 30 mins

Servings per Recipe: 8

| | |
|---|---|
| Calories | 392 kcal |
| Fat | 8.3 g |
| Carbohydrates | 53g |
| Protein | 27.4 g |
| Cholesterol | 42 mg |
| Sodium | 1139 mg |

## Ingredients

1 lb. dried pinto beans
1 lb. -lean ground beef
2 large sweet onions, diced
3 C. diced celery
3 carrots, peeled and diced
6 cloves garlic, minced
2 red bell peppers, diced
4 jalapeno peppers, seeded and minced
2 Anaheim peppers, seeded and diced
2 poblano peppers, seeded and diced
1 quart diced tomatoes

2 tbsp guajillo chile powder
1 1/2 tbsp ground cumin
1 tsp dried oregano
1 tsp ground coriander
1/4 tsp ground cinnamon
2 tbsp hot pepper sauce
1 tbsp beef bouillon granules
water, as needed
2 tsp salt

## Directions

1. In a large container, add the pinto beans and enough cool water to cover with several inches and keep aside for about 8 hours to overnight.

2. Heat a large pan on medium-high heat and cook the beef for about 7-10 minutes.

3. Drain the excess grease from the pan.

4. Drain the pinto beans and transfer into the pan.

5. Add the onions, celery, carrots, garlic, red bell peppers, jalapeño peppers, Anaheim peppers, poblano peppers, diced tomatoes, guajillo chile powder, cumin, oregano, coriander, cinnamon, hot pepper sauce and enough water.

6. Reduce the heat to medium-low and simmer for about 3 hours.

7. Stir in the beef granules and simmer for about 1-3 hours.

8. Season with the salt and serve.

# Spicy
# Honey Lamb

Prep Time: 45 mins
Total Time: 2 h 45 mins

Servings per Recipe: 4
Calories          616 kcal
Fat               18.4 g
Carbohydrates     82.9 g
Protein           39.1 g
Cholesterol       86 mg
Sodium            1135 mg

## Ingredients

2 tbsp olive oil
4 lamb shanks
1 onion, chopped
2 cloves garlic, minced
2 dried ancho chiles - chopped, stemmed and seeded
2 C. chicken broth
4 C. tomato puree
1 tsp ground cumin
1 bay leaf

salt and pepper to taste
6 dried ancho chiles, stemmed and seeded
4 C. boiling water
1/2 C. honey
1 tsp grated orange zest
1 C. plain yogurt
2 tbsp chopped fresh cilantro
salt to taste

## Directions

1. Set your oven to 350 degrees F before doing anything else.
2. In a large Dutch oven, heat the oil and sear the shanks till browned from all sides.
3. Transfer the shanks into a bowl and keep aside.
4. In the same pan, sauté the onion and garlic for about 2-3 minutes.
5. Stir in 2 ancho chilies, tomatoes, chicken stock, cumin, bay leaf, salt and pepper and bring to a gentle boil.
6. Add the shanks and stir to combine.
7. Cover the pan and transfer into the oven.
8. Cook in the oven for about 2-2 1/2 hours.
9. For the glaze in a bowl, soak 6 ancho chilies in the boiling water for about 10 minutes.
10. In a food processor, add the chilies, 1 C. of the water, honey and orange zest and pulse till smooth.
11. For the topping in a small bowl, mix together the yogurt, cilantro and salt.
12. Cover the bowl and refrigerate till serving.
13. Remove the shanks from the Dutch oven and place into a greased roasting pan.
14. Now, set your oven to 400 degrees F.
15. Spread the glaze over the shanks and cook in the oven for about 6-10 minutes.
16. Transfer the shanks into the large serving plates alongside the tomato base.
17. Serve with a topping of the yogurt mixture.

# 3-INGREDIENT
# Mesa Steaks

Prep Time: 5 mins
Total Time: 8 hr 15 mins

Servings per Recipe: 6
| | |
|---|---|
| Calories | 205 kcal |
| Fat | 11.7 g |
| Carbohydrates | 4.2g |
| Protein | 18.2 g |
| Cholesterol | 34 mg |
| Sodium | 330 mg |

## Ingredients
2 tbsp olive oil
2 (7 oz.) cans chipotle peppers
2 lb. flank steak

## Directions
1. In a blender, add the olive oil and chipotle peppers and pulse till smooth.
2. Coat the flank steak with the oil mixture generously and refrigerate to marinate for overnight.
3. Set your grill for medium-high heat and lightly, grease the grill grate.
4. Cook the flank steak on the grill for about 5 minutes per side.

# Cilantro and Tomato Pasta

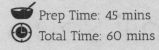 Prep Time: 45 mins
Total Time: 60 mins

Servings per Recipe: 4
Calories           540 kcal
Fat                27.5 g
Carbohydrates      59.7g
Protein            15.1 g
Cholesterol        138 mg
Sodium             484 mg

## Ingredients

1 tbsp olive oil
3 ancho chiles, stemmed and seeded
4 cloves unpeeled garlic
2 eggs
2 C. all-purpose flour
1/2 tsp salt
1 bunch chopped fresh cilantro
3 tomatillos, husked and chopped

1/2 jalapeno pepper, seeded and chopped
1/2 C. cream cheese, softened
1/2 C. sour cream
1/4 C. chicken stock
1 tbsp olive oil
1/2 tsp ground cumin
salt and pepper to taste

## Directions

1. In a skillet, heat 1 tbsp of the olive oil on medium-high heat and cook the ancho chiles and 4 unpeeled garlic cloves till begin to pop from both sides.
2. Transfer the chiles in a bowl of warm water and soak for about 30 minutes.
3. Cook the garlic for about 15 minutes, flipping occasionally.
4. Remove from the skillet and keep aside to cool.
5. Peel the garlic cloves.
6. In a food processor, add chiles, 2 roasted garlic cloves and eggs and pulse till smooth.
7. Place the flour and 1/2 tsp of the salt onto a clean surface and mix.
8. Make a well in the center of the flour mixture.
9. Add the egg mixture and with a fork, mix till a dough is formed.
10. With your hands, knead the dough for about 5 minutes.
11. Prepare the fettuccini according to your pasta machine's directions.
12. Arrange the fettuccine flat onto a lightly floured surface for about 15 minutes.
13. In a food processor, add remaining 2 garlic cloves, cilantro, tomatillos, jalapeño pepper, cream cheese, sour cream, chicken stock, 1 tbsp of the olive oil, cumin, salt and pepper and pulse till smooth.
14. Transfer the mixture into a pan on low heat and cook till heated completely.
15. In a large pan of the lightly salted boiling water, cook the fettuccini for about 2-3 minutes.
16. Drain well.
17. Divide the fettuccini into serving plates and serve with a topping of the sauce.

# COCONUT
# Chili Soup

Prep Time: 10 mins
Total Time: 20 mins

Servings per Recipe: 4

| | |
|---|---|
| Calories | 340 kcal |
| Fat | 12.8 g |
| Carbohydrates | 53.3g |
| Protein | 6.3 g |
| Cholesterol | 0 mg |
| Sodium | 968 mg |

## Ingredients

3 sweet potatoes, peeled and chopped
2 C. beef broth
1 C. unsweetened coconut milk
1 small shallot, minced
2 tbsp grade B maple syrup
2 tsp curry powder

1 tsp sea salt
1 tsp chili powder
1 tsp Spanish smoked paprika

## Directions

1. In a large pan, add the sweet potatoes and beef broth on medium-high heat and cook for about 5-10 minutes.

2. With a potato masher, mash the sweet potatoes into the broth.

3. In the pan, add the coconut milk, shallot, maple syrup, curry powder, salt, chili powder and paprika and cook for about 5-10 minutes, stirring occasionally.

4. Reduce the heat to low and with a hand blender, blend the soup till smooth.

5. Serve hot.

# *Arizona Sports Bar*
# Cream Cheese Dip

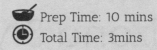

Prep Time: 10 mins
Total Time: 3mins

| Servings per Recipe: 32 | |
| --- | --- |
| Calories | 90 kcal |
| Fat | 7.2 g |
| Carbohydrates | 2g |
| Protein | < 10 |
| Cholesterol | 3 g |
| Sodium | 21 mg |

## Ingredients

1 (8 oz.) package cream cheese, softened
1/2 C. McCormick(R) Mayonnaise with Lime Juice
1/2 C. sour cream
1 (4 oz.) can diced green chilies, undrained
1 package McCormick(R) Burrito Seasoning Mix

1/2 C. shredded Mexican cheese blend, divided
1 1/2 C. shredded cooked chicken
2 6-inch tostada bowls

## Directions

1. Set your oven to 350 degrees F before doing anything else and line a baking sheet with a piece of the foil.
2. In a large bowl, add the cream cheese, mayonnaise, sour cream, chiles, Seasoning Mix and 1/4 C. of the shredded cheese and mix till well combined.
3. Stir in the chicken.
4. Arrange tostada bowls onto the prepared baking sheet.
5. Divide the dip into both tostada bowls evenly and sprinkle with remaining 1/4 C. of the shredded cheese.
6. Cook in the oven for about 25 minutes.

# POTATO SKINS
# Arizona Style

Prep Time: 20 mins
Total Time: 1 h 12 mins

Servings per Recipe: 4
| | |
|---|---|
| Calories | 277 kcal |
| Fat | 14.8 g |
| Carbohydrates | 27.2g |
| Protein | 10.4 g |
| Cholesterol | 38 mg |
| Sodium | 351 mg |

## Ingredients
Sauce:
1/2 C. sour cream
1/4 C. salsa verde
1 tbsp chopped fresh cilantro
Potatoes:
4 russet potatoes, peeled and chopped
8 poblano peppers
8 slices turkey bacon

1/2 red bell pepper, diced
1/2 onion, diced
2 cloves garlic, minced
1/2 C. shredded Cheddar cheese
1/2 C. milk
3 tbsp butter

## Directions
1. In a bowl, add the sour cream, salsa verde and cilantro and mix till well combined.
2. Refrigerate the sauce till serving.
3. In a large pan, add the potatoes and enough salted water to cover and bring to a boil.
4. Reduce the heat to medium-low and simmer for about 10 minutes.
5. Drain the potatoes and transfer into a large bowl to cool.
6. Set the broiler of your oven and arrange oven rack about 6-inch from the heating element.
7. Line a baking sheet with a piece of the foil.
8. Arrange the poblano peppers onto the prepared baking sheet.
9. Cook under the broiler for about 3-4 minutes.
10. Transfer the poblano peppers into a bowl and with a plastic wrap, seal tightly.
11. Keep aside for about 20 minutes.
12. Heat a large skillet on medium-high heat and cook the bacon for about 10 minutes, turning occasionally.
13. Transfer the bacon onto a paper towel lined plate to drain and then chop it.
14. Drain the bacon grease, leaving 1 tbsp in the skillet.
15. In the same skillet, add the red bell pepper, onion and garlic on medium heat and sauté for about 4-6 minutes.
16. In the bowl of the potatoes, add 1/2 of the bacon, bell pepper mixture, Cheddar cheese, milk and butter and mash till well combined.
17. Remove the skins from the roasted poblano peppers.
18. Make a small cut in each poblano pepper and scrape out the seeds.
19. Stuff the peppers with the potato mixture and serve with a topping of the remaining bacon and sauce.

# Sedona
# Style Tea

Prep Time: 10 mins
Total Time: 60 mins

Servings per Recipe: 1
| | |
|---|---|
| Calories | 262.3 |
| Fat | 0.0g |
| Cholesterol | 0.0mg |
| Sodium | 30.0mg |
| Carbohydrates | 68.8g |
| Protein | 0.1g |

## Ingredients

8 C. water
1 bag regular-size lipton green tea
1/2 C. granulated sugar

2 tbsp honey
3 tbsp lemon juice
1/4 tsp american ginseng extract

## Directions

1. In a pan, add water and bring to a boil.
2. Remove the pan from the heat and place the tea bag into the water.
3. Cover the pan and steep for about 1 hour.
4. In a large pitcher, place the sugar and honey.
5. Add the steeped tea and stir till the sugar dissolves completely.
6. Add remaining ingredients and stir to combine well.
7. Refrigerate to chill before serving.

# SWEET ONION
# Spuds

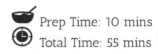

Prep Time: 10 mins
Total Time: 55 mins

| Servings per Recipe: 4 | |
| --- | --- |
| Calories | 378.8 |
| Fat | 23.2g |
| Cholesterol | 60.9mg |
| Sodium | 176.9mg |
| Carbohydrates | 40.0g |
| Protein | 4.8g |

## Ingredients

4 medium potatoes
1 sweet onion
4 oz. butter

salt, to taste
pepper, to taste
garlic powder, to taste

## Directions

1. Set your outdoor grill for medium-high heat.
2. Wash the potatoes and cut into 1/4-inch slices with skin intact.
3. Cut the onion into thin slices and then separate into the rings.
4. Place a 18-24-inch long piece of foil onto a smooth surface.
5. Place a layer of the potatoes in the center of foil piece, followed by a layer of the onion rings.
6. Sprinkle with the salt, pepper and a pinch of the garlic powder.
7. Repeat the layers, dotting each second layer with the butter.
8. Wrap the foil around the filling to make a parcel.
9. Cook the parcel on the grill for about 45-60 minutes.

# *Lemon Squares* Mesa

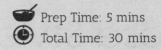

Prep Time: 5 mins

Total Time: 30 mins

Servings per Recipe: 21
| | |
|---|---|
| Calories | 133.8 |
| Fat | 6.2g |
| Cholesterol | 11.6mg |
| Sodium | 155.3mg |
| Carbohydrates | 16.4g |
| Protein | 3.5g |

## Ingredients

1/2 C. butter, whipped to double
2/3 C. Splenda granular
1 2/3 C. all-purpose flour
1 tsp salt
1 2/3 C. oats
1/4 C. almonds, chopped fine

3/4 C. lemon juice
zest of 2 large lemons
1 (14 oz.) cans fat-free sweetened condensed milk

## Directions

1. Set your oven to 350 degrees F before doing anything else and lightly, grease a 13x9-inch baking dish.
2. In a bowl, add the butter and Splenda and beat till creamy.
3. Add the flour, salt, oats, almonds and lemon zest and mix till a crumbly mixture is formed.
4. In another bowl, add the condensed milk and lemon juice and beat till well combined.
5. Place 1/2 of the crumbly mixture in the prepared baking dish and press lightly to smooth the surface.
6. Spread the milk mixture over the crumb mixture evenly.
7. Sprinkle with the remaining crumb mixture evenly and press lightly to smooth the surface.
8. Cook in the oven for about 25-30 minutes.
9. Remove from the oven and keep onto the wire rack to cool for about 1 hour.
10. Cut into 1 1/2-inch squares.
11. Serve warm.

# HOW TO MAKE
# Mesa Style Ribs

Prep Time: 30 mins

Total Time: 4 hr 30 mins

Servings per Recipe: 6
| | |
|---|---|
| Calories | 1537.4 |
| Fat | 100.0g |
| Cholesterol | 381.0mg |
| Sodium | 3558.4mg |
| Carbohydrates | 55.5g |
| Protein | 106.5g |

## Ingredients
6 lb. baby back ribs
1/4 C. paprika
2 tbsp kosher salt
1/2 C. firmly packed brown sugar
1/4 C. chili powder
5 - 6 garlic cloves, minced

2 tbsp ground cumin
1 tbsp dry mustard
1 tsp cayenne pepper
1 (16 oz.) bottles of your favorite barbecue sauce

## Directions
1. Carefully, remove the thin papery skin from the back of the ribs.
2. In a small bowl, mix together the paprika, salt, sugar, chili powder, garlic, cumin, mustard and cayenne pepper.
3. Rub the spice mixture over the ribs evenly.
4. Refrigerate, covered for about 4 hours or overnight.
5. Set your oven to 250 degrees F.
6. Arrange the ribs onto many sheet pans in a single layer, meat side up.
7. Cook in the oven for about 3 - 3 1/2 hours, flipping occasionally.
8. Remove the ribs from the oven and coat with the BBQ sauce generously.
9. Cook in the oven for about 30 minutes.

# *Mexican* Mushroom Chili

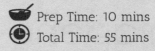 Prep Time: 10 mins
Total Time: 55 mins

Servings per Recipe: 6
| | |
|---|---|
| Calories | 457.5 |
| Fat | 12.4g |
| Cholesterol | 59.7mg |
| Sodium | 914.7mg |
| Carbohydrates | 59.9g |
| Protein | 33.4g |

## Ingredients

1 lb ground turkey
8 oz. mushrooms, sliced
2 (4 oz.) cans chopped green chilies
1 tbsp garlic, chopped
12 oz. tomato paste
3 (15 oz.) cans great northern beans,
drained and rinsed
7 oz. sun-dried tomatoes packed in oil,
drained and coarsely chopped
1 tsp dried thyme

1 tsp dried basil
1 tsp chili powder
1 tsp ground cumin
1 tsp cayenne pepper
1 tsp dried oregano
1 tsp paprika
3/4 tsp salt
chopped fresh cilantro ( to garnish)

## Directions

1. Heat a large nonstick skillet on medium-high heat and cook the turkey, mushrooms, chilies and garlic for about 10 minutes, stirring occasionally.
2. In a large pan, add the cooked turkey mixture, tomato paste, beans 6 C. of the water, sun dried tomatoes and all spices and bring to boil.
3. Reduce the heat to medium and simmer, uncovered for about 20 minutes, stirring occasionally.
4. Remove from the heat and keep aside for about 15 minutes before serving.
5. Serve with a garnishing of the cilantro.

# SPICE
# Jalapeno Pilaf

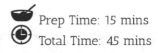

Prep Time: 15 mins
Total Time: 45 mins

Servings per Recipe: 4
| | |
|---|---|
| Calories | 310.4 |
| Fat | 11.7g |
| Cholesterol | 1.0mg |
| Sodium | 820.4mg |
| Carbohydrates | 44.7g |
| Protein | 7.0g |

## Ingredients
3 tbsp olive oil
1 onion, chopped
1 red pepper, chopped
1 carrot, chopped
1 stalk celery, chopped
1 C. long-grain white rice, uncooked

1 (14 1/2 oz.) cans beef broth
1 tomatoes, diced
1 large jalapeno chile, minced

## Directions
1. In a heavy large skillet. heat the oil on medium-high heat and sauté the onion, red pepper, carrot and celery for about 7 minutes.
2. Add the rice and stir to combine.
3. Add the broth and bring to a boil.
4. Reduce the heat to low and simmer, covered for about 20 minutes.
5. Stir in the tomato and jalapeño and simmer till heated completely.
6. Serve hot.

# *Tabasco* Salad

Prep Time: 15 mins
Total Time: 45 mins

Servings per Recipe: 4
| | |
|---|---|
| Calories | 272.9 |
| Fat | 22.4g |
| Cholesterol | 0.0mg |
| Sodium | 34.7mg |
| Carbohydrates | 19.5g |
| Protein | 4.8g |

## Ingredients

3 avocados, seeded and peeled
1 tbsp onion, minced
1 tsp lemon juice
1/2 tsp chili powder
1/8 tsp cumin

2 drops Tabasco sauce
salt
4 medium ripe tomatoes
8 lettuce leaves

## Directions

1. Peel the tomatoes and remove the top.
2. Carefully, scoop out the pulp to make a cup.
3. Peel he the avocados and remove the pit.
4. Chop the avocado and transfer into a bowl.
5. Add the lemon juice and toss to coat well.
6. Add the onion, chili, cumin, Tabasco sauce and salt and mix.
7. Stuff the tomatoes with the avocado mixture evenly.
8. Refrigerate to chill for at least 1/2 hour.
9. Serve each tomato over the lettuce.

# EASY
# Southwest Ribs

Prep Time: 10 mins
Total Time: 30 mins

Servings per Recipe: 2
Calories           12.8
Fat                0.2g
Cholesterol        0.0mg
Sodium             2.5mg
Carbohydrates      3.1g
Protein            0.4g

## Ingredients

1 lime, juice of
1 tsp minced garlic
1 tsp dried oregano
1 tsp ground cumin
1 (7 oz.) cans chipotle chiles in adobo

2 lb. top sirloin steaks
salt and pepper

## Directions

1. Chop the chile peppers finely.
2. With a sharp knife, pierce the steaks several times and season with the salt and pepper to taste.
3. In a large bowl, mix together the lime juice, garlic, oregano, cumin, chile peppers and some adobo sauce.
4. add the steaks and coat with the marinade generously
5. Refrigerate, covered for about 1-2 hours.
6. Set your outdoor grill for high heat and lightly, grease the frill grate.
7. Cook the steak on the grill till desired doneness.

# Arizona Navy Bean Dinner

🥣 Prep Time: 20 mins
🕐 Total Time: 10 hr 20 mins

Servings per Recipe: 12
Calories            357.5
Fat                 19.3g
Cholesterol         47.2mg
Sodium              563.8mg
Carbohydrates       26.4g
Protein             19.8g

## Ingredients

1 lb dried navy beans
6 C. water
1 large onion, chopped
1 clove garlic, minced
1 large green bell pepper, chopped
1 1/2 lb. chuck steaks, cubed
1 1/2 tsp salt

1/2 tsp oregano, crumbled
1/4 tsp red pepper
1/4 tsp ground cumin
8 oz. tomato sauce

## Directions

1. Pick over the beans and rinse under running cold water well.
2. In a large kettle, add the beans and water and bring to a boil.
3. Cook, covered for about 2 minutes.
4. Remove from the heat and keep aside for about 1 hour.
5. Transfer the beans with water into a crock pot.
6. Heat a large skillet and cook the salt pork till browned completely.
7. In the same skillet, sauté the onion, garlic and green pepper till tender.
8. With a slotted spoon, transfer the onion mixture into the crock pot.
9. In the same skillet, cook the beef in batches till browned completely.
10. With a slotted spoon, transfer the beef into the crock pot.
11. Add the salt, oregano, red pepper, cumin and tomato sauce and stir to combine.
12. Set the crock pot on High and cook, covered for about 6 hours.

# EASY
# Southwest Ribs

Prep Time: 10 mins
Total Time: 30 mins

Servings per Recipe: 2
Calories            12.8
Fat                 0.2g
Cholesterol         0.0mg
Sodium              2.5mg
Carbohydrates       3.1g
Protein             0.4g

## Ingredients

1 lime, juice of
1 tsp minced garlic
1 tsp dried oregano
1 tsp ground cumin

1 (7 oz.) cans chipotle chiles in adobo
2 lb. top sirloin steaks
salt and pepper

## Directions

1. Chop the chile peppers finely.
2. With a sharp knife, pierce the steaks several times and season with the salt and pepper to taste.
3. In a large bowl, mix together the lime juice, garlic, oregano, cumin, chile peppers and some adobo sauce.
4. add the steaks and coat with the marinade generously
5. Refrigerate, covered for about 1-2 hours.
6. Set your outdoor grill for high heat and lightly, grease the frill grate.
7. Cook the steak on the grill till desired doneness.

# Southwest
# Egg Scramble

Prep Time: 20 mins
Total Time: 40 mins

Servings per Recipe: 2
| | |
|---|---|
| Calories | 498.9 |
| Fat | 27.4g |
| Cholesterol | 248.4mg |
| Sodium | 1628.1mg |
| Carbohydrates | 34.6g |
| Protein | 28.6g |

## Ingredients

1 C. whole milk
2 large eggs
1/2 tsp salt
1/2 tsp pepper
1 C. monterey jack cheese, grated
3 tbsp green onions, sliced

2 tsp jalapeno peppers, minced
2 C. white bread, cubed
1/2 C. chunky salsa
2 tbsp fresh cilantro, chopped

## Directions

1. Set your oven to 400 degrees F before doing anything else and lightly, grease a 9-inch pie dish.
2. In bowl, add the milk, eggs, salt and pepper and beat till well combined.
3. Add the cheese, green onion, and jalapeño pepper and bread cubes and stir till moistened.
4. Transfer the mixture into the prepared pie dish even and keep aside for about 5 minutes, pressing several times.
5. Cook in the oven for about 20 minutes or till a toothpick inserted in the center comes out clean.
6. In a small bowl, mix together the salsa and cilantro.
7. Cut the strata into desired sized wedges and serve alongside the salsa.

# SOUTHWEST
# Lemonade

Prep Time: 5 mins
Total Time: 5 mins

Servings per Recipe: 7
Calories            173.0
Fat                 0.0g
Cholesterol         0.0mg
Sodium              2.9mg
Carbohydrates       45.1g
Protein             0.2g

## Ingredients
3 lemons
1 1/2 C. sugar
2 C. water ( filtered)

## Directions
1. Remove the ends of 2 lemons and cut each into 8 pieces.
2. In a blender, add the lemon pieces with the seeds, juice of remaining lemon, 2 C. of the water and sweetener of your choice and pulse well.
3. Strain the juice into a container and stir in 5 C. of the water.
4. Serve chilled

# *Mesa*
# Shrimp and Rice

Prep Time: 10 mins
Total Time: 30 mins

Servings per Recipe: 4
| | |
|---|---|
| Calories | 1483.8 |
| Fat | 18.5g |
| Cholesterol | 477.9mg |
| Sodium | 4745.2mg |
| Carbohydrates | 262.2g |
| Protein | 78.5g |

## Ingredients

4 C. water
5 whole tomatoes
2 medium red onions, divided
6 garlic cloves
1 (14 oz.) canned chipotle peppers
24 oz. ketchup

1 tsp salt
2 tbsp canola oil
2 lb. shrimp, shelled and deveined
1/2 tsp garlic salt
10 C. cooked white rice

## Directions

1. In a large pan, add the water, tomatoes, half an onion and garlic cloves on high heat and bring to a boil.
2. Reduce heat and simmer till the tomatoes become soft.
3. Remove from the heat and keep aside to cool for about 2 minutes.
4. In a blender, add the chipotle, ketchup and salt and pulse for at least 30 seconds.
5. Mince the remaining 1 1/2 of the onions.
6. In a large sauté pan, heat the oil on medium-high heat and sauté the onion till golden brown.
7. Stir in the shrimp and garlic salt and cook for about 2 minutes.
8. Place the sauce over the shrimp and simmer for about 5-8 minutes.
9. Serve the shrimp mixture over the rice.

# CHIPOTLE
# Cheesecake

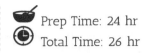

Prep Time: 24 hr
Total Time: 26 hr

Servings per Recipe: 6
| | |
|---|---|
| Calories | 1694.7 |
| Fat | 91.5g |
| Cholesterol | 388.5mg |
| Sodium | 676.6mg |
| Carbohydrates | 203.1g |
| Protein | 24.3g |

## Ingredients

Crust:
1 1/2 C. flour
1/2 C. finely ground pecans
1/3 C. sugar
1 large egg, separated
1/2 C. butter, softened
Fruit Filing:
1 can whole berry cranberry sauce
2 tbsp sugar
1 tbsp cornstarch
1 tbsp grated lemon, zest of
1 tbsp lemon juice
Chocolate Filling:
1 1/2 C. fresh orange juice
3 inches orange rind, by 1 inch wide ( no

white part)
32 oz. cream cheese, softened
2/3 C. sugar
1 tbsp grated orange zest
2 tbsp cranberry juice,
8 oz. white chocolate, melted
4 eggs
Sweet Garnish
4 C. water
2 C. sugar
3 seedless oranges, unpeeled, cut into paper-thin slices
fresh whipped cream

## Directions

1. Set your oven to 400 degrees F before doing anything else.
2. For the shortbread crust, place the flour, pecans and sugar in the center of the large smooth surface and mix well.
3. Make a well in the center of the flour mixture.
4. Add the egg yolk and the softened butter in the well and with your hands, mix till a dough is formed.
5. Make a ball from the dough and cover with a plastic wrap.
6. Refrigerate to chill for at least 10 minutes.
7. Place the dough onto a lightly floured surface and roll into 1/4-inch thick and 11-inch in diameter circle.
8. Carefully, cut the crust in a 9-inch circle.
9. Arrange the circle inside a 9-inch spring form pan.
10. With a fork, prick the crust several times.

11. Cook in the oven for about 15-20 minutes.
12. Remove from the oven and keep aside to cool.
13. With the leftover dough, line the sides of the spring form pan and press to smooth the surface and side crust meets the bottom crust all the way around.
14. Coat the bottom and sides of the crust with the the reserved egg white evenly and keep aside.
15. For the glaze filling in a small pan, mix together the sugar, cornstarch and cranberry sauce on medium heat and cook till the mixture becomes thick, stirring continuously.
16. Stir in the lemon zest and lemon juice and remove from the heat.
17. Keep aside to cool slightly.
18. Set your oven to 350 degrees F.
19. For the chocolate filling in a heavy medium pan, add the orange juice and piece of orange peel and cook for about 12 minutes, stirring occasionally.
20. Remove and discard the orange peel piece and keep aside to cool slightly.
21. In a large bowl, add the cream cheese, sugar, grated orange zest, Crantasia, cooked orange juice and with an electric mixer, beat till smooth.
22. Add the melted white chocolate and beat till well combined.
23. Add the eggs, one at a time, beating till just combined.
24. Spread the glaze filling in the prepared crust evenly and top with the chocolate filling.
25. Cook in the oven for about 50 minutes.
26. Remove from the oven and keep onto the wire rack to cool completely in the room temperature.
27. Refrigerate to chill for overnight.
28. For the oranges topping with a waxed paper, cover a wire rack and keep aside.
29. In a heavy shallow wide skillet, mix together the water and sugar on medium heat and cook till the sugar is dissolved.
30. Simmer for about 5 minutes.
31. Add the orange slices, 1 at a time and adjust the heat so that the syrup bubbles slightly.
32. Cook for about 1 hour.
33. Turn over the top layer of oranges and cook for about 1 hour more.
34. Remove each orange slice from the syrup and drain completely.
35. Arrange the orange slices onto the prepared rack in a single layer and keep aside to dry for about 1 hour.
36. Boil the orange syrup for about 6 minutes.
37. Carefully, remove the sides of the spring form pan.
38. Place the cheesecake onto a serving dish and arrange the candied orange slices over the top of the cheesecake.
39. Coat the orange slices with the orange syrup.

# SCOTTSDALE
# Stuffing

Prep Time: 1 hr
Total Time: 7 hr

Servings per Recipe: 8
| | |
|---|---|
| Calories | 211.1 |
| Fat | 19.1g |
| Cholesterol | 98.6mg |
| Sodium | 671.8mg |
| Carbohydrates | 6.3g |
| Protein | 5.2g |

## Ingredients

3/4 C. unsalted butter
2 medium yellow onions, chopped
2 C. chopped celery
1 lb fresh white mushroom, sliced
12 1/2 C. packed stale white bread cubes
1/4 C. chopped fresh Italian parsley
1 1/2 tsp poultry seasoning
1 1/2 tsp salt
2 tsp crumbled dried sage

1 tsp crumbed dried thyme
1/2 tsp dried marjoram
1/2 tsp fresh ground black pepper
2 - 3 C. chicken broth
2 large eggs, beaten

## Directions

1. In a large skillet, melt the butter on medium heat.
2. Reserve some butter for greasing the crock pot.
3. In the skillet, cook the onions, celery and mushrooms for about 15 minutes.
4. In a large bowl, add the bread, parsley, poultry seasoning, salt, sage, thyme, marjoram and pepper and toss to coat.
5. Add the sautéed vegetables and mix well.
6. In another bowl, add the broth and the eggs and beat till well combined.
7. Add enough broth over the stuffing and mix till the mixture becomes moist.
8. Grease a crock pot with some melted butter generously.
9. Place the stuffing into the crock pot lightly.
10. Set the crock pot on High and cook, covered for about 1 hour.
11. Now, set the crock pot on Low and cook, covered for about 4-5 hours.
12. Now, set the crock pot on Keep Warm mode for about 2-3 hours before serving.
13. Serve hot.

# Hubbell
# Chipped Beef Spread

Prep Time: 10 mins
Total Time: 10 mins

| Servings per Recipe: 6 | |
|---|---|
| Calories | 223.7 |
| Fat | 18.0g |
| Cholesterol | 68.6mg |
| Sodium | 701.4mg |
| Carbohydrates | 3.8g |
| Protein | 12.2g |

## Ingredients

2 (8 oz.) packages light cream cheese, softened
6 radishes
6 green onions

3 oz. chipped beef (Jarred)(jerky)
2 tbsp water

## Directions

1. Set your oven to 400 degrees F before doing anything else and lightly, grease a 9-inch pie dish.
2. In bowl, add the milk, eggs, salt and pepper and beat till well combined.
3. Add the cheese, green onion, and jalapeño pepper and bread cubes and stir till moistened.
4. Transfer the mixture into the prepared pie dish even and keep aside for about 5 minutes, pressing several times.
5. Cook in the oven for about 20 minutes or till a toothpick inserted in the center comes out clean.
6. In a small bowl, mix together the salsa and cilantro.
7. Cut the strata into desired sized wedges and serve alongside the salsa.

# CHIPOTLE
# Cornbread

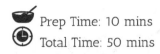

Prep Time: 10 mins
Total Time: 50 mins

Servings per Recipe: 4

| | |
|---|---|
| Calories | 439.7 |
| Fat | 28.3g |
| Cholesterol | 92.5mg |
| Sodium | 965.6mg |
| Carbohydrates | 36.1g |
| Protein | 14.6g |

## Ingredients

1 (16 oz.) cans creamed corn
1 egg, beaten
1/2 C. cornmeal
1/2 tsp garlic salt
1/4 C. salad oil

1/4 tsp baking powder
1 (4 oz.) cans diced green chilies
1/3 lb grated longhorn cheese, divided

## Directions

1. Set your oven to 350 degrees F before doing anything else and grease a casserole dish.
2. In a bowl, add all the ingredients except 2 handfuls of the cheese and mix till well combined.
3. Transfer the mixture into the prepared casserole dish and sprinkle with the remaining cheese.
4. Cook in the oven for about 40 minutes.

# Spicy Puebla Wontons

Prep Time: 15 mins
Total Time: 1 hr 45 mins

Servings per Recipe: 18
Calories              169.5
Fat                   5.8g
Cholesterol           25.6mg
Sodium                269.7mg
Carbohydrates         18.9g
Protein               9.5g

## Ingredients

1 lb ground beef
1/2 C. chopped onion
1 (15 oz.) cans refried beans
2/3 C. shredded cheddar cheese
2 tbsp picante sauce

1 tsp chili powder
1/4 tsp ground cumin
1 (1 lb) package wonton skins
oil ( for deep frying)

## Directions

1. Heat a large skillet on and cook the beef and onion till browned completely.
2. Drain the excess grease from the skillet and transfer the beef mixture into a bowl.
3. In the bowl of the beef mixture, add the beans, cheese, picante sauce, chili powder and cumin and mix well.
4. Refrigerate for about 1 hour.
5. Arrange won-ton skin onto a plate with 1 point toward you.
6. Place a tsp of the mixture over the center of the skin.
7. Fold the bottom point over and tuck under filling.
8. Fold the side corners over to form an envelope.
9. Fold over top corner and with wet fingers, moisten the point to seal.
10. Repeat with the remaining skins and beef mixture.
11. In a deep skillet, heat the oil to 400 degrees F and fry the Wontons in batches for about 2 minutes.
12. Serve immediately.

# CILANTRO DIJON
# Chicken Cutlets

🥣 Prep Time: 10 mins

🕐 Total Time: 30 mins

Servings per Recipe: 4

| | |
|---|---|
| Calories | 173.0 |
| Fat | 6.1g |
| Cholesterol | 83.1mg |
| Sodium | 399.1mg |
| Carbohydrates | 2.8g |
| Protein | 25.7g |

## Ingredients

4 boneless skinless chicken breast halves
1 tbsp Dijon mustard
1 tbsp butter
1/2 C. prepared salsa

2 tbsp fresh lime juice
1/4 C. chopped fresh cilantro

## Directions

1. Arrange each chicken breast between 2 plastic wrap sheets and with a meat mallet, pound into 1/2-inch thickness.
2. Spread mustard over each breast.
3. In a large skillet, melt the butter on medium heat and cook the chicken for about 3-4 minutes per side.
4. Stir in the salsa and lime juice and simmer, uncovered for about 6-8 minutes.
5. Serve with a sprinkling of the cilantro.

# Ranch Style
# Chili

🥘 Prep Time: 10 mins
🕐 Total Time: 1 hr 10 mins

Servings per Recipe: 8
Calories           298.0
Fat                20.3g
Cholesterol        78.2mg
Sodium             883.8mg
Carbohydrates      8.0g
Protein            21.5g

## Ingredients

2 lb. ground chuck
1 C. chopped onion
1 garlic clove, minced
1 1/2 tsp salt
1 tsp paprika

1 tsp oregano
3/8 C. chili powder
1 (15 oz.) cans tomato sauce
2 C. water
1 (16 oz.) cans ranch-style pinto beans

## Directions

1. Heat a large pan on and cook the beef, onion, garlic and seasonings till browned completely.
2. Stir in the remaining ingredients and simmer for at least 1 hour.

# MARIA'S
# 6-ingredient Chili

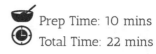 Prep Time: 10 mins

Total Time: 22 mins

Servings per Recipe: 4

| | |
|---|---|
| Calories | 328.6 |
| Fat | 4.8g |
| Cholesterol | 56.6mg |
| Sodium | 142.8mg |
| Carbohydrates | 45.5g |
| Protein | 30.4g |

## Ingredients

3 boneless skinless chicken breasts
1 (14 1/2 oz.) cans diced tomatoes ( with peppers and onions)
1 tbsp chili powder
1 (15 oz.) cans black beans, drained and

rinsed
1 (15 oz.) cans corn, drained
1/4 C. fresh cilantro, chopped

## Directions

1. Cut the chicken into 1/2-inch chunks.

2. In a medium pan, mix together the chicken, undrained tomatoes and chili powder on medium heat and cook for about 5 minutes.

3. Add the remaining ingredients and simmer for about 5-7 minutes.

# Southwest
# Corn Chip Salad

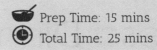

Prep Time: 15 mins
Total Time: 25 mins

Servings per Recipe: 16
Calories          481.9
Fat               27.1g
Cholesterol       60.8mg
Sodium            662.1mg
Carbohydrates     38.3g
Protein           22.8g

## Ingredients

1 head iceberg lettuce, cut up, torn up, shredded
2 lb. ground beef
4 C. pinto beans, drained
20 oz. Fritos corn chips
4 -6 green onions, sliced

1 (6 oz.) cans sliced black olives
4 -6 tomatoes, cut into bite-sized chunks
12 oz. pre-shredded cheddar cheese
12 oz. Pace Picante Sauce, medium spicy
1 oz. hot sauce

## Directions

1. Heat a large skillet and cook the beef, salt, pepper and garlic till browned completely.
2. Remove from the heat and keep aside to cool.
3. In a bowl, mix together the beef, beans and lettuce.
4. Divide the corn chips, green onions, black olives, tomato chunks, Cheddar cheese and beef mixture.
5. Top with the picanté sauce and hot sauce and serve.

# FULL
# Mesa Dinner
# (Monterey Macaroni)

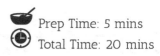

Prep Time: 5 mins

Total Time: 20 mins

| | |
|---|---|
| Servings per Recipe: 4 | |
| Calories | 593.0 |
| Fat | 16.0g |
| Cholesterol | 18.4mg |
| Sodium | 592.4mg |
| Carbohydrates | 91.0g |
| Protein | 26.7g |

## Ingredients

2 tbsp olive oil
1 medium yellow onion, chopped
1 medium green bell pepper, chopped
2 garlic cloves, minced
2 tbsp chili powder
1/2 tsp ground cumin
1 (16 oz.) cans kidney beans, drained and rinsed

1 (10 oz.) frozen whole kernel corn, thawed
2 (16 oz.) cans low-tomatoes, with liquid and chopped
1 (8 oz.) packages macaroni, uncooked
1 (4 oz.) packages low-fat Monterey jack cheese, shredded

## Directions

1. In a large pan of the lightly salted boiling water, prepare the macaroni according to the package's directions.
2. Drain well and transfer into a bowl.
3. In a large skillet, heat the oil on medium-high heat and sauté the onion, green pepper, garlic, chili powder and cumin for about 5 minutes.
4. Add the kidney beans, corn and tomatoes with liquid and bring to a boil.
5. Reduce the heat to low and simmer for about 15 minutes, stirring occasionally.
6. Transfer the beans mixture into the bowl of the cooked macaroni and toss to coat well.
7. Serve with a sprinkling of the Monterey jack cheese..

# Queen
# Rancho Soup

Prep Time: 1 hr
Total Time: 1 hr

| Servings per Recipe: 6 | |
|---|---|
| Calories | 336.2 |
| Fat | 19.8g |
| Cholesterol | 12.5mg |
| Sodium | 1090.4mg |
| Carbohydrates | 31.4g |
| Protein | 14.0g |

## Ingredients

4 corn tortillas ( 6 to 7 in.)
3 tbsp salad oil
1 onion, peeled and finely chopped
1 dried bay leaf
1/2 tsp dried oregano
1/2 tsp black peppercorns
1/2 tsp hot chili flakes
8 C. fat-skimmed chicken broth
1 avocado ( about 8 oz.)
1 lime ( about 3 oz.)

3/4 C. shredded monterey jack cheese
salt and pepper
salsa fresca
1 lb tomatoes
1 fresh jalapeno
1/4 C. finely chopped onion
1/4 C. chopped fresh cilantro
3 tbsp lime juice
salt and pepper

## Directions

1. Cut the tortillas into 1-inch-wide strips.
2. In a 5-6-quart pan, heat the oil on high heat and cook the tortilla strips for about 2-3 minutes, stirring occasionally.
3. Transfer the tortilla strips onto the paper towels lined plate to drain.
4. In the same pan, add the onion and garlic on medium-high heat and sauté for about 3-4 minutes.
5. Stir in the bay leaf, oregano, peppercorns, chili flakes and broth and bring to a boil on high heat.
6. Cook for about 20-25 minutes.
7. Meanwhile for the salsa, rinse and core the tomatoes.
8. Cut each tomato into 1/4-inch pieces and transfer into a bowl with their juices.
9. Rinse the jalapeño pepper and remove the stems and seeds.
10. Then, cut out the veins and chop it finely.
11. In the bowl of the tomatoes, add the jalapeño pepper, onion, cilantro, 3 tbsp of the lime

juice, salt and pepper and gently, stir to combine.

12. In a blender, add half of the salsa and pulse till puréed roughly.

13. Add the puréed salsa into hot soup with the salt and pepper and stir to combine.

14. Pit, peel and thinly slice the avocado.

15. Cut the lime into thin slices crosswise and discard the ends.

16. In wide soup bowls, divide the tortilla strips, remaining salsa, avocado slices, lime slices, and jack cheese.

17. Top with the soup and serve.

# Mi Tiga's Stew

 Prep Time: 30 min

Total Time: 2 h 30 mins

Servings per Recipe: 12

| | |
|---|---|
| Calories | 511 kcal |
| Fat | 31.2 g |
| Carbohydrates | 34.4g |
| Protein | 23.7 g |
| Cholesterol | 96 mg |
| Sodium | 804 mg |

## Ingredients

3 lb. ground beef
2 large onions, diced
2 tbsp chili powder
6 potatoes, diced
1 lb. carrots, diced
3 C. white hominy
3 (8 oz.) cans whole peeled tomatoes with

liquid, chopped
2 (4 oz.) cans chopped green chiles, with juice
3 C. beef broth
1/2 tsp salt
1/2 tsp ground black pepper

## Directions

1. Heat a large skillet on medium heat and cook the beef till browned completely.

2. Stir in the onions and sauté till soft and translucent.

3. Stir in the chili powder and cook for about 2 minutes.

4. Stir in the potatoes, carrots, hominy, tomatoes, chilies, beef broth, salt and pepper.

5. Reduce the heat and simmer for about 2 hours.

# HUEVOS RANCHEROS
## (Mesa Scrambled Eggs)

Prep Time: 10 mins
Total Time: 20 mins

Servings per Recipe: 4
| | |
|---|---|
| Calories | 494 kcal |
| Fat | 32.9 g |
| Carbohydrates | 24.2g |
| Protein | 26.6 g |
| Cholesterol | 247 mg |
| Sodium | 1194 mg |

## Ingredients
2 tbsp vegetable oil
4 (6 inch) corn tortillas
1 C. refried beans with green chilies
1 tsp butter
4 eggs

1 C. shredded Cheddar cheese
8 slices turkey bacon, cooked and crumbled
1/2 C. salsa

## Directions
1. In a small skillet, heat the oil on medium-high heat and fry tortillas, one at a time till firm.
2. Transfer the tortillas onto a paper towel lined plate to drain.
3. Meanwhile in a microwave safe dish, place the refried beans and butter and microwave, covered till heated completely.
4. In the same skillet, fry the eggs till desired doneness.
5. Place each tortilla onto 1 plate.
6. Place a layer of beans over each tortilla and top with cheese, a fried egg, crumbled bacon and salsa.

# *How to Make* Chimichangas

🥄 Prep Time: 10 min
🕐 Total Time: 3 h 10 mins

Servings per Recipe: 4
| | |
|---|---|
| Calories | 714 kcal |
| Fat | 46.6 g |
| Carbohydrates | 35.9g |
| Protein | 38 g |
| Cholesterol | 151 mg |
| Sodium | 1176 mg |

## Ingredients

2 lb. boneless beef chuck roast, trimmed of fat
1/4 C. water
1 1/2 C. beef broth
3 tbsp red wine vinegar
2 tbsp chili powder

1 tsp ground cumin
4 (8 inch) flour tortilla
3 tbsp butter, melted
1 C. salsa
1/2 C. shredded Monterey Jack cheese
1/2 C. sour cream

## Directions

1. In a Dutch oven, add the beef and water on medium heat and cook, covered for about 30 minutes.
2. Uncover and cook for about 10 minutes.
3. In a bowl, mix together the beef broth, red wine vinegar, chili powder and cumin.
4. Place the broth mixture over the beef and cook, covered for about 2 hours.
5. Remove from the heat and keep aside to cool.
6. Shred the beef and mix with pan juices.
7. Set your oven to 500 degrees F.
8. Coat both sides of each tortilla with the melted butter.
9. Place the shredded beef in the center of each tortilla.
10. Fold ends over the filling and then fold sides to center to make a packet.
11. Place burritos in a 13x9-inch baking dish, seam side down.
12. Cook in the oven for about 8-10 minutes.
13. Serve these burritos alongside the shredded cheese, sour cream and salsa.

# VEGETARIAN
# Mesa Quesadillas

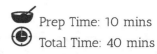 Prep Time: 10 mins

Total Time: 40 mins

Servings per Recipe: 8

| | |
|---|---|
| Calories | 363 kcal |
| Fat | 14.5 g |
| Carbohydrates | 45.6 g |
| Protein | 13.9 g |
| Cholesterol | 26 mg |
| Sodium | 732 mg |

## Ingredients

2 tsp olive oil
3 tbsp finely chopped onion
1 (15.5 oz.) can black beans, drained and rinsed
1 (10 oz.) can whole kernel corn, drained
1 tbsp brown sugar
1/4 C. salsa

1/4 tsp red pepper flakes
2 tbsp butter, divided
8 (8 inch) flour tortillas
1 1/2 C. shredded Monterey Jack cheese, divided

## Directions

1. In a large pan, heat the oil on medium heat and sauté the onion for about 2 minutes.
2. Stir in the beans, corn, sugar, salsa and pepper flakes and cook for about 3 minutes.
3. In a large skillet, melt 2 tsp of the butter on medium heat.
4. Place 1 tortilla in the skillet and sprinkle evenly with the cheese.
5. Top with some of the bean mixture and cover with another tortilla.
6. Cook till the bottom of tortillas becomes golden brown from both sides.
7. Repeat with the remaining tortillas and filling.

# Quesadillas
# Sedona

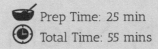 Prep Time: 25 min

Total Time: 55 mins

| Servings per Recipe: 4 | |
| --- | --- |
| Calories | 673 kcal |
| Fat | 29.1 g |
| Carbohydrates | 72.8g |
| Protein | 31 g |
| Cholesterol | 65 mg |
| Sodium | 979 mg |

## Ingredients

2 tomatoes, diced
1 onion, finely chopped
2 limes, juiced
2 tbsp chopped fresh cilantro
1 jalapeño pepper, seeded and minced
salt and pepper to taste
2 tbsp olive oil, divided
2 skinless, boneless chicken breast halves

- cut into strips
1/2 onion, thinly sliced
1 green bell pepper, thinly sliced
2 cloves garlic, minced
4 (12 inch) flour tortillas
1 C. shredded Monterey Jack cheese
1/4 C. sour cream, for topping

## Directions

1. In a small bowl, mix together the tomatoes, onion, lime juice, cilantro, jalapeño pepper, salt and pepper.
2. In a large skillet, heat 1 tbsp of the olive oil and sear the chicken till cooked through.
3. Transfer the chicken into a plate and keep aside.
4. In the same skillet, heat the remaining 1 tbsp of the olive oil and sauté the sliced onion and green pepper till tender.
5. Stir in the minced garlic and sauté till aromatic.
6. Stir in half of the pico de gallo and cooked chicken.
7. Keep aside, covered to keep the mixture warm.
8. In a heavy skillet, heat 1 flour tortilla.
9. Spread 1/4 C. of the shredded cheese over the tortilla, followed by 1/2 of the chicken mixture and 1/4 C. of the cheese.
10. Cover with another tortilla.
11. Cook till the bottom of tortillas becomes golden brown from both sides.
12. Remove the quesadilla from the skillet and cut into quarters.
13. Repeat with the remaining tortillas and filling.
14. Serve quesadillas with the sour cream and remaining pico de gallo.

# ARIZONA
# City Sirloin

Prep Time: 15 mins
Total Time: 2 h 30 mins

Servings per Recipe: 4
| | |
|---|---|
| Calories | 342 kcal |
| Fat | 18.8 g |
| Carbohydrates | 3.7g |
| Protein | 37.6 g |
| Cholesterol | 120 mg |
| Sodium | 429 mg |

## Ingredients
1 lime, juiced
1 tbsp minced garlic
1 tsp dried oregano
1 tsp ground cumin
2 tbsp finely chopped canned chipotle
peppers in adobo sauce
adobo sauce from canned chipotle peppers

to taste
4 (8 oz.) beef sirloin steaks
salt and pepper to taste

## Directions
1. With a sharp knife, pierce the steaks on both sides and season with the salt and black pepper.
2. In a glass bowl, mix together the lime juice, garlic, oregano and cumin.
3. Stir in the chipotle peppers and adobo sauce.
4. Add the steaks and coat with the mixture generously.
5. Cover and refrigerate for about 1-2 hours.
6. Set your grill for high heat and lightly, grease the grill grate.
7. Remove the steaks from the bowl and discard the marinade.
8. Cook the steaks on the grill for about 6 minutes per side.

# *Fried Bread*
# from Arizona

Prep Time: 30 min
Total Time: 60 mins

Servings per Recipe: 8
| | |
|---|---|
| Calories | 479 kcal |
| Fat | 29 g |
| Carbohydrates | 48g |
| Protein | 6.5 g |
| Cholesterol | 0 mg |
| Sodium | 418 mg |

## Ingredients
4 C. all-purpose flour
1 tbsp baking powder
1 tsp salt
4 tbsp shortening

1 1/3 C. cold water
2 quarts oil for deep frying

## Directions
1. In a large bowl, sift together the flour, baking powder and salt.
2. With a pastry blender, cut the shortening till a coarse crumbs like mixture is formed.
3. Add the cold water and with your hands, mix till a smooth dough is formed.
4. Place the dough onto a floured surface and knead for about 5 minutes.
5. Divide the dough into 8 equal sized portions and shape each one into round balls.
6. Cover the balls and keep aside.
7. Place each dough ball onto a lightly floured surface and flatten into 1/2-inch thick lunch plate sized circle.
8. In a deep fryer, heat the oil to 375 degrees F and fry the dough in batches till browned from both sides.
9. With a slotted spoon, transfer the dough onto a paper towel lined plate to drain.

# OLD RANCH
# Road Salad

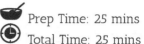 Prep Time: 25 mins
Total Time: 25 mins

Servings per Recipe: 6

| | |
|---|---|
| Calories | 391 kcal |
| Fat | 24.5 g |
| Carbohydrates | 35.1g |
| Protein | 10.5 g |
| Cholesterol | 0 mg |
| Sodium | 830 mg |

## Ingredients

1/3 C. fresh lime juice
1/2 C. olive oil
1 clove garlic, minced
1 tsp salt
1/8 tsp ground cayenne pepper
2 (15 oz.) cans black beans, rinsed and drained

1 1/2 C. frozen corn kernels
1 avocado - peeled, pitted and diced
1 red bell pepper, chopped
2 tomatoes, chopped
6 green onions, thinly sliced
1/2 C. chopped fresh cilantro

## Directions

1. In a small jar, add the lime juice, olive oil, garlic, salt and cayenne pepper.
2. Cover the jar with the lid tightly and shake till all ingredients are well combined.
3. In a salad bowl, mix together the beans, corn, avocado, bell pepper, tomatoes, green onions and cilantro.
4. Shake the dressing and pour over the salad.
5. Gently, stir to combine and serve immediately.

# *Baked* Burritos

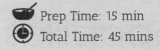 Prep Time: 15 min

Total Time: 45 mins

Servings per Recipe: 6

| | |
|---|---|
| Calories | 916 kcal |
| Fat | 42 g |
| Carbohydrates | 92g |
| Protein | 43.9 g |
| Cholesterol | 122 mg |
| Sodium | 2285 mg |

## Ingredients

1 lb. ground beef
1/2 C. chopped onion
1 clove garlic, minced
1/2 tsp cumin
1/4 tsp salt
1/8 tsp pepper
1 (4.5 oz.) can diced green chile peppers
1 (16 oz.) can refried beans

1 (15 oz.) can chili without beans
1 (10.75 oz.) can condensed tomato soup
1 (10 oz.) can enchilada sauce
6 (12 inch) flour tortillas, warmed
2 C. shredded lettuce
1 C. chopped tomatoes
2 C. shredded Mexican blend cheese
1/2 C. chopped green onions

## Directions

1. Heat a large skillet on medium-high heat and cook the beef till browned completely.
2. Add the onion and cook till translucent.
3. Drain the grease from the skillet.
4. In the skillet, add the garlic, cumin, salt, pepper, green chilies and refried beans and stir till well combined.
5. Turn off the heat but keep the skillet, covered on stove to keep the mixture warm.
6. In a pan, mix together the chili without beans, tomato soup and enchilada sauce on medium heat and cook till heated completely.
7. Turn off the heat but keep the skillet, covered on stove to keep the mixture warm.
8. Arrange each warmed tortilla onto a plate.
9. Place about 1/2 C. of the beef mixture in the center of each tortilla and top with lettuce and tomato.
10. Roll up the tortillas over the filling tightly.
11. Place a generous amount of the sauce over each tortilla and sprinkle with the cheese and green onions.
12. Arrange the Tortillas onto a microwave safe plate and microwave for about 30 seconds.

# ROSA'S
# Sopapillas

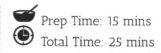

Prep Time: 15 mins
Total Time: 25 mins

Servings per Recipe: 12
Calories          127 kcal
Fat               6 g
Carbohydrates     16.1g
Protein           2.2 g
Cholesterol       0 mg
Sodium            254 mg

## Ingredients
2 C. all-purpose flour
2 tsp baking powder
1 tsp salt
2 tbsp shortening

3/4 C. water
2 C. vegetable oil for frying

## Directions
1. In a large bowl, sift together the flour, baking powder and salt.
2. With a pastry blender, cut the shortening till a coarse crumbs like mixture is formed.
3. Add the water and with your hands, mix till a smooth dough is formed.
4. Place the dough onto a floured surface and knead slightly.
5. Divide the dough into 12 equal sized portions and shape each one into round balls.
6. Cover the balls and keep aside.
7. Place each dough ball onto a lightly floured surface and roll into thin circles.
8. Cut each circle into equal sized triangles.
9. In a deep-fryer, heat the oil to 375 degrees F and fry the dough triangles till golden brown, turning when the dough puffs.
10. With a slotted spoon, transfer the dough triangles onto a paper towel lined plate to drain.

# *Arizona*
# Style Cabbage

Prep Time: 6 min
Total Time: 10 mins

Servings per Recipe: 3

| | |
|---|---|
| Calories | 174.7 |
| Fat | 13.7g |
| Cholesterol | 20.5mg |
| Sodium | 278.9mg |
| Carbohydrates | 8.6g |
| Protein | 5.6g |

## Ingredients

4 -5 slices turkey bacon, cut across the slice to make small pieces
1/2 head cabbage, chopped into bite size pieces
salt and pepper

## Directions

1. Heat a large skillet on medium-high heat and cook the bacon till cooked completely.
2. Stir in the cabbage and cook till wilted, stirring occasionally.
3. Stir in the salt and black pepper and serve.

# MESA
# Macaroni Salad

Prep Time: 10 mins
Total Time: 20 mins

Servings per Recipe: 4
| | |
|---|---|
| Calories | 534.8 |
| Fat | 24.8g |
| Cholesterol | 15.2mg |
| Sodium | 1501.3mg |
| Carbohydrates | 72.7g |
| Protein | 10.9g |

## Ingredients

2 C. small shell pasta
1 C. mayonnaise
2 C. chunky salsa
1 tbsp chopped fresh cilantro
6 green onions, chopped
1 C. cooked corn

1 C. sliced black olives
1 red pepper, chopped
1/2 tsp onion salt
1/4 tsp cayenne pepper

## Directions

1.  In a large pan of the lightly salted boiling water, prepare the pasta according to the package's directions.
2.  Drain well.
3.  In a large bowl add the remaining ingredients and mix till well combined.
4.  Add the pasta and toss to coat.
5.  Refrigerate to chill before serving.

# Laguna Seca Burritos

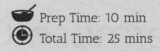

Prep Time: 10 min

Total Time: 25 mins

Servings per Recipe: 2

| | |
|---|---|
| Calories | 692 kcal |
| Fat | 35.8 g |
| Carbohydrates | 70.2g |
| Protein | 21.2 g |
| Cholesterol | 47 mg |
| Sodium | 1803 mg |

## Ingredients

2 (10 inch) flour tortillas
2 tbsp vegetable oil
1 small onion, chopped
1/2 red bell pepper, chopped
1 tsp minced garlic
1 (15 oz.) can black beans, rinsed and

drained
1 tsp minced jalapeño peppers
3 oz. cream cheese
1/2 tsp salt
2 tbsp chopped fresh cilantro

## Directions

1. Set your oven to 350 degrees F before doing anything else.
2. With the pieces of foil, wrap each tortilla in foil.
3. Cook in the oven for about 15 minutes.
4. In a 10-inch skillet, heat the oil on medium heat and cook the onion, bell pepper, garlic and jalapeño for about 2 minutes, stirring occasionally.
5. Stir in the beans and cook for about 3 minutes, stirring continuously.
6. Cut the cream cheese into cubes.
7. Add the cubed ream cheese into the skillet and cook for abort 2 minutes, stirring occasionally.
8. Stir in the cilantro and remove from the heat.
9. Place the beans mixture in the center of each tortilla evenly and roll tightly like a burrito.
10. Serve immediately.

# RANCHA
# Hermosa Chili

Prep Time: 15 mins
Total Time: 1 h 15 mins

Servings per Recipe: 8
| | |
|---|---|
| Calories | 391 kcal |
| Fat | 7.9 g |
| Carbohydrates | 58.7g |
| Protein | 28.2 g |
| Cholesterol | 0 mg |
| Sodium | 2571 mg |

## Ingredients

1 tbsp olive oil
1/2 medium onion, chopped
2 bay leaves
1 tsp ground cumin
2 tbsp dried oregano
1 tbsp salt
2 stalks celery, chopped
2 green bell peppers, chopped
2 jalapeno peppers, chopped
3 cloves garlic, chopped
2 (4 oz.) cans chopped green chile peppers, drained

2 (12 oz.) packages vegetarian burger crumbles
3 (28 oz.) cans whole peeled tomatoes, crushed
1/4 C. chili powder
1 tbsp ground black pepper
1 (15 oz.) can kidney beans, drained
1 (15 oz.) can garbanzo beans, drained
1 (15 oz.) can black beans
1 (15 oz.) can whole kernel corn

## Directions

1.  In a large pan, heat the oil on medium heat and sauté the onion, bay leaves, cumin, oregano and salt till the onion becomes tender.
2.  Stir in the celery, bell peppers, jalapeño peppers, garlic and green chile peppers and cook till heated completely.
3.  Stir in the vegetarian burger crumbles.
4.  Reduce the heat to low and simmer, covered for about 5 minutes.
5.  Stir in the tomatoes, chili powder, pepper and beans and bring to a boil.
6.  Reduce the heat to low and simmer for about 45 minutes.
7.  Stir in the corn and simmer for about 45 minutes.

# *Arizona*
# Hummus

Prep Time: 15 min
Total Time: 30 mins

Servings per Recipe: 2
| | |
|---|---|
| Calories | 90 kcal |
| Fat | 3.7 g |
| Carbohydrates | 11.9g |
| Protein | 2.9 g |
| Cholesterol | 0 mg |
| Sodium | 235 mg |

## Ingredients

2 (15.5 oz.) cans garbanzo beans, drained
1/2 C. water
1/4 C. tahini (sesame-seed paste)
1/4 C. fresh lemon juice
2 tbsps olive oil
1 canned chipotle pepper in adobo sauce
2 cloves garlic
1 1/2 tsps cumin

1 (7 oz.) jar roasted red bell peppers, drained
6 oil-packed sun-dried tomatoes, drained
1/2 C. chopped cilantro
1/2 tsp salt
ground black pepper to taste

## Directions

1. In a food processor, add beans, tahini, chipotle pepper, garlic, oil and lemon juice and pulse till well combined and smooth.
2. Add the remaining ingredients and pulse till chopped finely.
3. Place the hummus in a bowl and refrigerate, covered before serving.

# BARBECUED
# Meatloaf

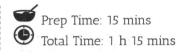
Prep Time: 15 mins
Total Time: 1 h 15 mins

Servings per Recipe: 8
Calories           306 kcal
Fat                16.2 g
Carbohydrates      12.7g
Protein            25.8 g
Cholesterol        124 mg
Sodium             635 mg

## Ingredients
2 eggs
1/3 C. hickory flavored barbeque sauce
2 cloves garlic, minced, or to taste
2 chipotle chilies in adobo sauce, minced, or to taste
2 tbsps adobo sauce from chipotle peppers
1 tsp kosher salt
1 tsp coarse ground black pepper

1/2 tsp celery salt
1/2 tsp ground cumin
1 tbsp Worcestershire sauce
1 onion, chopped
1/2 C. dry oatmeal
2 pounds lean ground beef
2 tbsps hickory flavored barbeque sauce

## Directions
1. Set your oven to 350 degrees F before doing anything else and grease a 9x5-inch loaf pan.
2. In a large bowl, crack the eggs and beat till smooth.
3. Add 1/3 C. of barbecue sauce, adobo sauce, Worcestershire sauce, chipotle chilis, garlic, cumin, celery salt, kosher salt and black pepper and beat till well combined.
4. Add beef, oatmeal and onion and mix till well combined and transfer into the prepared loaf pan evenly and coat the top with the remaining barbecue sauce.
5. Cook in the oven for about 1 hour or till done completely.

# Chipotle
# Mac and Cheese

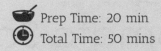 Prep Time: 20 min

Total Time: 50 mins

Servings per Recipe: 10

| | |
|---|---|
| Calories | 556 kcal |
| Fat | 31.5 g |
| Carbohydrates | 44.2g |
| Protein | 23.3 g |
| Cholesterol | 98 mg |
| Sodium | 986 mg |

## Ingredients

1 pound elbow macaroni, cooked according to package directions
Sauce:
1 quart half and half, divided
1 chipotle pepper from canned chipotles in adobo sauce, or more to taste
5 chicken bouillon cubes
3 cloves fresh garlic, roughly chopped
1 tbsp Spice Islands(R) Onion Powder

1/2 tsp Spice Islands(R) Fine Grind Black Pepper (optional)
1/4 C. Argo(R) OR Kingsford's(R) Corn Starch
2 C. shredded Monterey Jack cheese
2 C. shredded pepperjack cheese
Topping:
1 C. shredded pepper jack cheese OR sprinkle with Spice Islands(R) Paprika

## Directions

1. Set your oven to 350 degrees F before doing anything else and grease a 13x9-inch casserole dish.
2. In a food processor or blender, add half-and-half, chipotle peppers, garlic and bouillon and pulse till well combined.
3. Transfer the mixture into a large pan with the remaining half-and-half, cornstarch, onion powder and black pepper.
4. Bring to a boil, stirring continuously and boil for about 1 minute or till thick and immediately remove from heat.
5. Immediately, add cheese and stir till melted completely and then stir in the cooked macaroni.
6. Transfer the mixture into the prepared casserole dish evenly and top with the desired topping evenly.
7. Cook everything in the oven for about 25-30 minutes or till the top becomes bubbly and golden brown.

# CHIPOTLE
# Tomato Salsa

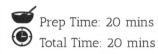

Prep Time: 20 mins
Total Time: 20 mins

Servings per Recipe: 8
| | |
|---|---|
| Calories | 14 kcal |
| Fat | 0.2 g |
| Carbohydrates | 3.2g |
| Protein | 0.5 g |
| Cholesterol | 0 mg |
| Sodium | 299 mg |

## Ingredients

1 (14.5 oz.) can whole peeled tomatoes
1 fresh jalapeno pepper, seeded
1 chipotle chili in adobo sauce, seeded
1 (1 inch) piece dried ancho chili pepper
1 clove garlic
2 1/2 tbsps chopped onion
1 tbsp chopped fresh cilantro

1 tbsp lemon juice, or to taste
3/4 tsp salt
1/4 tsp white sugar, or to taste
1/4 tsp ground cumin

## Directions

1. In a blender, add all the ingredients and pulse till desired consistency.
2. Transfer into a bowl and keep aside till the flavors blend completely.

# Sweet & Spicy Mustard Chicken Thighs

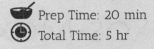

Prep Time: 20 min
Total Time: 5 hr

| Servings per Recipe: 8 | |
| --- | --- |
| Calories | 352 kcal |
| Fat | 19 g |
| Carbohydrates | 13.8g |
| Protein | 29.1 g |
| Cholesterol | 106 mg |
| Sodium | 765 mg |

## Ingredients

8 large bone-in, skin-on chicken thighs
1/2 C. Dijon mustard
1/4 C. packed brown sugar
1/4 C. red wine vinegar
1 tsp dry mustard powder
1 tsp salt

1 tsp freshly ground black pepper
1/2 tsp ground dried chipotle pepper
1 pinch cayenne pepper, or to taste
4 cloves garlic, minced
1 onion, sliced into rings
2 tsps vegetable oil, or as needed

## Directions

1. With a sharp knife, cut 2 (1-inch apart) slashes into the skin and meat to the bone of the chicken thighs crosswise.
2. In a large bowl, mix together all the ingredients except onion and oil and transfer the mixture into a large resealable bag.
3. Add the chicken thighs and shake the bag to coat with marinade evenly and seal the bag tightly.
4. Refrigerate to marinate for about 4-8 hours.
5. Set your oven to 450 degrees F before doing anything else and line a large baking sheet with a lightly greased piece of foil.
6. Spread the onion rings onto the prepared baking sheet evenly and top with chicken thighs.
7. Coat the thighs with oil and sprinkle with seasoning if you like.
8. Cook in the oven for about 35-45 minutes or till done completely.
9. In a large serving platter, place thighs and onion rings.
10. In a small pan, add the baking sheet drippings and cook, stirring occasionally for about 3-4 minutes or till it reduces to half.
11. Serve the chicken and onion rings with the topping of pan sauce.

# AUTHENTIC
# Texas-Mexican Enchiladas

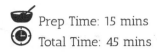

Prep Time: 15 mins
Total Time: 45 mins

| Servings per Recipe: 5 | |
| --- | --- |
| Calories | 933 kcal |
| Fat | 59 g |
| Carbohydrates | 69.1g |
| Protein | 35.1 g |
| Cholesterol | 108 mg |
| Sodium | 1776 mg |

## Ingredients

2 (11.25 oz.) cans chili without beans
1 C. enchilada sauce
1/2 C. vegetable oil
1 tbsp chili powder

15 corn tortillas
1 lb. shredded Cheddar cheese
1 onion, chopped

## Directions

1. Set your oven to 350 degrees F before doing anything else.
2. In a small pan, mix the chili and enchilada sauce on medium-low heat and heat, stirring occasionally.
3. In a small skillet, heat the vegetable oil and chili powder on medium heat and cook the tortillas, one at a time till they start to puff.
4. Transfer the tortillas on a plate and immediately sprinkle with 1/4 C. of the Cheddar cheese and 1 tbsp of the chopped onion in the center of each tortilla.
5. Roll the tortillas tightly around the mixture and place, seam-side down, into the bottom of a 13x9-inch baking dish.
6. Sprinkle about 2/3 of the remaining Cheddar cheese over the rolled enchiladas.
7. Place the warm chili mixture over the enchiladas evenly, followed by the remaining Cheddar cheese.
8. Cook in the oven for about 20-25 minutes.

# *Sweet and Spicy* Mustard Chicken Thighs

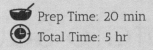 Prep Time: 20 min

Total Time: 5 hr

Servings per Recipe: 8

| | |
|---|---|
| Calories | 352 kcal |
| Fat | 19 g |
| Carbohydrates | 13.8g |
| Protein | 29.1 g |
| Cholesterol | 106 mg |
| Sodium | 765 mg |

## Ingredients

8 large bone-in, skin-on chicken thighs
1/2 C. Dijon mustard
1/4 C. packed brown sugar
1/4 C. red wine vinegar
1 tsp dry mustard powder
1 tsp salt

1 tsp freshly ground black pepper
1/2 tsp ground dried chipotle pepper
1 pinch cayenne pepper, or to taste
4 cloves garlic, minced
1 onion, sliced into rings
2 tsps vegetable oil, or as needed

## Directions

1. With a sharp knife, cut 2 (1-inch apart) slashes into the skin and meat to the bone of the chicken thighs crosswise.
2. In a large bowl, mix together all the ingredients except onion and oil and transfer the mixture into a large resealable bag.
3. Add the chicken thighs and shake the bag to coat with marinade evenly and seal the bag tightly.
4. Refrigerate to marinate for about 4-8 hours.
5. Set your oven to 450 degrees F before doing anything else and line a large baking sheet with a lightly greased piece of foil.
6. Spread the onion rings onto the prepared baking sheet evenly and top with chicken thighs.
7. Coat the thighs with oil and sprinkle with seasoning if you like.
8. Cook in the oven for about 35-45 minutes or till done completely.
9. In a large serving platter, place thighs and onion rings.
10. In a small pan, add the baking sheet drippings and cook, stirring occasionally for about 3-4 minutes or till it reduces to half.
11. Serve the chicken and onion rings with the topping of pan sauce.

# LONE STAR STATE
# Potato Soup

 Prep Time: 20 mins

Total Time: 55 mins

Servings per Recipe: 6

| | |
|---|---|
| Calories | 219 kcal |
| Fat | 13.2 g |
| Carbohydrates | 17.7g |
| Protein | 8.2 g |
| Cholesterol | 69 mg |
| Sodium | 379 mg |

## Ingredients

2 potatoes, peeled and cubed
1 onion, chopped
1 green bell pepper, chopped
1 red bell pepper, chopped
2 tbsp margarine
4 oz. chopped ham
1 tbsp chopped green chili peppers
1/4 tsp ground white pepper

1/8 tsp cayenne pepper
1 (14.5 oz.) can chicken broth
1 egg yolk, beaten
1/4 C. heavy whipping cream
1/2 C. shredded Cheddar cheese

## Directions

1. In a pan of boiling water, cook the potatoes for about 15 minutes.
2. Drain and keep aside.
3. In a skillet, melt the margarine and sauté the onion and bell peppers for about 10 minutes.
4. Stir in the turkey, green chilies, white pepper and cayenne and sauté for about 1 minute.
5. In a blender, add the potatoes and chicken broth and pulse till smooth.
6. Add the potato mixture into the ham mixture and bring to a boil.
7. In a small bowl, add the egg yolk and heavy cream and beat to combine.
8. Stir in 1/2 C. of the hot soup.
9. Stir the yolk mixture into the soup and cook till heated completely.
10. Serve with a garnishing of the shredded cheddar cheese.

# Catalina's
# Stir Fry

Prep Time: 20 min
Total Time: 35 min

Servings per Recipe: 4
| | |
|---|---|
| Calories | 333 kcal |
| Fat | 15.9 g |
| Carbohydrates | 13.3g |
| Protein | 32.1 g |
| Cholesterol | 94 mg |
| Sodium | 945 mg |

## Ingredients
1 tsp olive oil
1 green bell pepper, chopped
1 red bell pepper, chopped
2 tbsp all-purpose flour
1 (1 oz.) packet taco seasoning mix
1 lb. skinless, boneless chicken breast
halves - cut into bite size pieces
2 tsp olive oil
1 (15 oz.) can black beans, rinsed and drained
1/2 C. prepared salsa
1 C. shredded Cheddar cheese

## Directions
1. In a skillet, heat 1 tsp of the olive oil on medium-high heat and sauté the bell peppers for about 5 minutes.
2. Remove from the heat and keep aside.
3. In a bowl, mix together the flour and taco seasoning in a bowl.
4. Coat the chicken pieces with the flour mixture evenly.
5. In a large skillet, heat 2 tsp of the olive oil on medium-high heat and cook the chicken for about 5 minutes.
6. Stir in the bell peppers, black beans and salsa and simmer for about 5 minutes.
7. Serve with a sprinkling of the Cheddar cheese.

# QUINOA SALAD
# from Mexico

Prep Time: 20 mins
Total Time: 2 h 40 mins

Servings per Recipe: 10
| | |
|---|---|
| Calories | 219 kcal |
| Fat | 11.1 g |
| Carbohydrates | 25.7g |
| Protein | 6.3 g |
| Cholesterol | 3 mg |
| Sodium | 515 mg |

## Ingredients

1 C. quinoa
2 C. water
1 tsp kosher salt
1/4 C. fresh lime juice
2 tbsp olive oil
1/8 tsp ground black pepper
1 (14 oz.) can diced tomatoes with green chili peppers, drained

1 (14 oz.) can garbanzo beans, drained and rinsed
1 bunch cilantro, chopped
2 avocados, cubed
1/4 C. crumbled cotija cheese

## Directions

1. In a pan, add the quinoa, water and salt and bring to a boil.
2. Reduce the heat to medium-low and simmer, covered for about 20-25 minutes.
3. Meanwhile in a large bowl, mix together the lime juice, olive oil, pepper, diced tomatoes and garbanzo beans.
4. Add the quinoa and stir to combine.
5. Refrigerate to cool for about 2 hours.
6. With a fork, fluff the quinoa mixture and gently fold in the cilantro, avocados and cheese.

# *Tex Mex*
# Breakfast Eggs

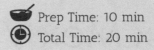 Prep Time: 10 min

Total Time: 20 min

| Servings per Recipe: 6 | |
|---|---|
| Calories | 283 kcal |
| Fat | 12.2 g |
| Carbohydrates | 30.8g |
| Protein | 12.1 g |
| Cholesterol | 196 mg |
| Sodium | 661 mg |

## Ingredients

1 tbsp butter
1 (4 oz.) can chopped green chilis
1/2 tomato, chopped
6 large eggs

1/4 C. crushed tortilla chips
1/4 C. shredded sharp Cheddar cheese
6 (8 inch) flour tortillas
6 tbsp taco sauce

## Directions

1. In a large skillet, melt the butter on medium heat and cook the green chilis and tomato for about 5 minutes.
2. Carefully, crack the eggs into the skillet and stir till the yolks break.
3. Cook, stirring for about 2-3 minutes.
4. Sprinkle the tortilla chips on top and mix with the eggs.
5. Move egg mixture to the side of the skillet and remove from the heat.
6. Immediately, sprinkle the Cheddar cheese over the egg mixture and keep aside, covered for about 5 minutes.
7. In a microwave-safe plate, place the flour tortillas and microwave for about 30 seconds.
8. Divide the egg mixture onto each tortilla and serve with a topping of the taco sauce.

# AUGUST'S
# Tex Mex Veggie Casserole

 Prep Time: 30 mins

Total Time: 1 h 10 mins

Servings per Recipe: 8
Calories                281 kcal
Fat                     15.8 g
Carbohydrates           20g
Protein                 17 g
Cholesterol             39 mg
Sodium                  298 mg

## Ingredients
1 lb. ground beef
1/4 C. olive oil, divided
4 zucchini, cut into 1/2-inch cubes
1 red bell pepper, chopped
1 jalapeno pepper, seeded and chopped
4 cloves garlic, minced
4 green onions, chopped -- white and green parts separated
salt and pepper to taste

3 tbsp tomato paste
4 tsp chili powder
2 tsp ground cumin
1 (15 oz.) can black beans, rinsed and drained
1 (15 oz.) can kidney beans, rinsed and drained
1 C. frozen corn, thawed
1/2 C. grated Parmesan cheese, divided
1/4 C. chopped fresh cilantro

## Directions
1. Set your oven to 400 degrees F before doing anything else and grease a 13x9-inch baking dish with about 1 tsp of the olive oil.
2. Heat a large skillet on medium heat and cook the beef for about 10 minutes.
3. Drain the excess grease from the skillet and keep aside.
4. Meanwhile in another large skillet, heat the remaining olive oil on medium-high heat and cook the zucchini, red bell pepper, jalapeño pepper, garlic and white parts of the green onions for about 3-5 minutes.
5. Stir in the salt, black pepper, tomato paste, chili powder and cumin and simmer for about 1 minute.
6. Remove from the heat.
7. Add the cooked ground beef, black beans, kidney beans, corn and 1/4 C. of the Parmesan cheese and stir till well combined.
8. Transfer the mixture into the prepared baking dish evenly and top with the remaining 1/4 C. of the Parmesan cheese.
9. With a foil paper, cover the baking dish and cook in the oven for about 20-25 minutes.
10. Remove the foil paper and cook in the oven for about 5-10 minutes.
11. Serve with a garnishing of the remaining green onions (green tops) and cilantro.

# *Tilapia*
# South of the Border

Prep Time: 20 min
Total Time: 1 h 28 min

Servings per Recipe: 4
| | |
|---|---|
| Calories | 225 kcal |
| Fat | 14.9 g |
| Carbohydrates | 4.8g |
| Protein | 18.3 g |
| Cholesterol | 31 mg |
| Sodium | 141 mg |

## Ingredients

4 (3 oz.) fresh tilapia fillets
1/4 C. olive oil
1/4 C. fresh lime juice
2 tomatoes, chopped

2 fresh jalapeno peppers, sliced into rings
8 sprigs cilantro leaves
salt and ground black pepper to taste

## Directions

1.  In a glass baking dish, arrange the tilapia fillets.
2.  Drizzle with the olive oil and lime juice evenly and season with the salt and pepper.
3.  Keep in the room temperature for about 1 hour.
4.  In a non-stick skillet, place the tilapia fillets on medium heat.
5.  Pour the lime juice mixture from the baking dish on top.
6.  Arrange the tomatoes, jalapeños and cilantro over the fillets and cook for about 4 minutes per side.

# CATALINA'S
# Salad

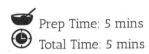 Prep Time: 5 mins
Total Time: 5 mins

Servings per Recipe: 10
| | |
|---|---|
| Calories | 542 kcal |
| Fat | 33.1 g |
| Carbohydrates | 52.7g |
| Protein | 10.7 g |
| Cholesterol | 12 mg |
| Sodium | 1077 mg |

## Ingredients

1 (15 oz.) can pinto beans, drained and rinsed
1 (15 oz.) can black beans, rinsed and drained
1 1/2 C. shredded Cheddar and Monterey cheese blend

1 (10 oz.) package chopped romaine lettuce
3 tomatoes, chopped
1 (16 oz.) bottle Catalina salad dressing
1 (16 oz.) package corn chips

## Directions

1.  In a large bowl, mix together the pinto beans, black beans, cheese, lettuce and tomatoes.
2.  Add 3/4 of the bottle of the dressing and mix well.
3.  Add the corn chips before serving.

# Nacharito
# Bake

Prep Time: 15 min
Total Time: 1 h 30 min

Servings per Recipe: 4
Calories            480 kcal
Fat                 29.5 g
Carbohydrates       31.1g
Protein             24.2 g
Cholesterol         71 mg
Sodium              1209 mg

## Ingredients

1 (10 oz.) bag nacho cheese-flavored corn chips, crushed
1 tbsp butter
1 small onion, finely chopped
1 (14.5 oz.) can diced tomatoes
1 (10.75 oz.) can condensed cream of chicken soup
1 (10.75 oz.) can cream of mushroom soup

1 (4.5 oz.) can chopped green chilis
1/3 C. milk
2 tbsp sour cream
1 tsp chili powder
1 tsp ground cumin
2 1/2 C. chopped cooked chicken
1 (8 oz.) package shredded sharp Cheddar cheese

## Directions

1. Set your oven to 350 degrees F before doing anything else and lightly, grease a 13x9-inch baking dish.
2. Spread the corn chip crumbs in the bottom of the prepared baking dish and press downwards.
3. In a large skillet, melt the butter on medium-high heat and sauté the onion for about 6-7 minutes.
4. In a large bowl, add the diced tomatoes, cream of chicken soup, cream of mushroom soup, green chilis, milk, sour cream, chili powder, cumin, chicken and cooked onion and stir to combine.
5. Place the mixture over the corn chips evenly and top with the Cheddar cheese.
6. Cook in the oven for about 55-60 minutes.
7. Remove from the oven and keep aside for about 10 minutes before serving.

# LA ÁGUILA
# Dip

 Prep Time: 20 mins

Total Time: 1 hr

Servings per Recipe: 12
| | |
|---|---|
| Calories | 390 kcal |
| Fat | 29.8 g |
| Carbohydrates | 11.5g |
| Protein | 19.1 g |
| Cholesterol | 84 mg |
| Sodium | 925 mg |

## Ingredients

1 lb. ground beef
1 tsp chili powder
1 (16 oz.) can vegetarian refried beans
1 yellow onion, chopped
2 (4 oz.) cans chopped green chili peppers, drained
1 (16 oz.) jar picante sauce

1/2 lb. Muenster cheese, cubed
1/2 lb. Monterey Jack cheese, cubed
1 (16 oz.) container sour cream
5 pieces turkey bacon

## Directions

1. Set your oven to 350 degrees F before doing anything else.
2. Heat a large skillet on medium-high heat and cook the bacon till browned completely.
3. Drain the excess grease from the skillet.
4. Stir in the chili powder and cook for about 5 minutes.
5. In an 8x8-inch baking dish, spread the refried beans, followed by the ground beef mixture, onion, green chili peppers, picante sauce, Muenster cheese and Monterey Jack cheese.
6. Cook in the oven for about 35-45 minutes.
7. Serve with a topping of the sour cream.

# October's
# Tex Mex Soup

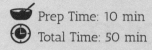 Prep Time: 10 min

Total Time: 50 min

Servings per Recipe: 6
| | |
|---|---|
| Calories | 684 kcal |
| Fat | 30.5 g |
| Carbohydrates | 59.2g |
| Protein | 45.7 g |
| Cholesterol | 112 mg |
| Sodium | 2036 mg |

## Ingredients

1 tbsp olive oil
1/2 C. minced onion
3 cloves garlic, minced
2 tsp chili powder
1/2 tsp cumin
1/2 tsp oregano
4 C. water
1 (10.75 oz.) can condensed tomato soup
1 (28 oz.) can diced tomatoes
1 C. salsa
4 C. shredded cooked turkey
1 tbsp dried parsley
3 chicken bouillon cubes

1 (14 oz.) can black beans, rinsed, drained
2 C. frozen corn
1/2 C. sour cream
1/4 C. chopped fresh cilantro
Toppings:
6 C. corn tortilla chips
3/4 C. chopped green onion
1 C. shredded Cheddar-Monterey Jack cheese blend
1/2 C. chopped fresh cilantro
1/2 C. sour cream

## Directions

1. In a large pan, heat the olive oil on medium heat and sauté the minced onions for about 4 minutes.
2. Add the garlic, chili powder, cumin and oregano and sauté for about 1 minute.
3. Stir in the water, tomato soup, diced tomatoes, salsa, shredded turkey, parsley and bouillon cubes and bring to a boil.
4. Reduce the heat and simmer for about 5 minutes.
5. Add the black beans, corn, sour cream and cilantro and simmer for about 20-30 minutes.
6. Serve the soup with a topping of the crushed tortilla chips, chopped green onion, shredded cheese, additional cilantro and sour cream.

# A TRUE TEXAN
# Cake

Prep Time: 30 mins
Total Time: 45 mins

Servings per Recipe: 15
| | |
|---|---|
| Calories | 449 kcal |
| Fat | 22.8 g |
| Carbohydrates | 57.7g |
| Protein | 7 g |
| Cholesterol | 32 mg |
| Sodium | 379 mg |

## Ingredients

2 C. all-purpose flour
1 1/2 C. brown sugar
1 tsp baking soda
1 tsp ground cinnamon
1/2 tsp salt
1 C. margarine
1 C. water
1/4 C. unsweetened cocoa powder
1 tbsp instant coffee granules

1/3 C. sweetened condensed milk
2 eggs
1 tsp vanilla extract
1/4 C. margarine
1/4 C. unsweetened cocoa powder
1 tbsp instant coffee granules
2/3 C. sweetened condensed milk
1 C. confectioners' sugar
1 C. slivered, toasted almonds

## Directions

1. Set your oven to 350 degrees F before doing anything else and grease a 15x10-inch jelly roll pan.
2. In a bowl, mix together the flour, baking soda, brown sugar, cinnamon and salt.
3. In a small pan, melt 1 C. of the margarine.
4. Stir in the water, 1/4 C. of the cocoa and 1 tbsp of the instant coffee and bring to a boil.
5. Remove from the heat.
6. Make a well in the center of the flour mixture.
7. Place the cocoa mixture in the well of the flour mixture.
8. Add 1/3 C. of the sweetened condensed milk, eggs and vanilla and mix till well combined.
9. Transfer the mixture into the prepared pan.
10. Cook in the oven for about 15-20 minutes.
11. Remove from the oven and keep aside to cool.
12. For the coffee glaze in a small pan, melt 1/4 C. of the margarine.
13. Add 1/4 C. of the cocoa, 1 tbsp of the instant coffee and sweetened condensed milk, and confectioners' sugar and stir to combine.
14. Fold in the almonds.
15. Spread the glaze over the warm cake.

# Tuesday's
# San Miguel Potatoes

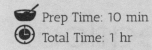 Prep Time: 10 min
🕐 Total Time: 1 hr

Servings per Recipe: 4
| | |
|---|---|
| Calories | 420 kcal |
| Fat | 13.2 g |
| Carbohydrates | 60.3g |
| Protein | 17.2 g |
| Cholesterol | 25 mg |
| Sodium | 681 mg |

## Ingredients
4 baking potatoes
1 tbsp vegetable oil
1 onion, chopped
1 large green bell pepper, chopped
1 tsp minced garlic
1 (16 oz.) can chili beans in spicy sauce,
undrained
1 tbsp vegetarian Worcestershire sauce
1/2 tsp minced jalapeno peppers
1 C. shredded Monterey Jack cheese

## Directions
1. With a sharp knife, scrub the potatoes and prick in several places.
2. Place the potatoes onto a paper towel and arrange in a microwave and microwave on high for about 8 minutes.
3. Turn and rotate the potatoes and microwave for about 8-10 minutes.
4. In a medium skillet, heat the oil on medium-high heat and sauté the onions and bell peppers till softened.
5. Stir in the beans, Worcestershire sauce, and jalapeño peppers.
6. Reduce the heat to low and simmer, covered for about 5-6 minutes.
7. Split the potatoes and top with the bean mixture.
8. Serve with a sprinkling of the cheese.

# PUERTO VALLARTA X HOUSTON
# Meatloaf

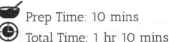

Prep Time: 10 mins
Total Time: 1 hr 10 mins

| Servings per Recipe: 4 | |
| --- | --- |
| Calories | 711 kcal |
| Fat | 56.9 g |
| Carbohydrates | 9.8g |
| Protein | 39.2 g |
| Cholesterol | 264 mg |
| Sodium | 1605 mg |

## Ingredients

1 1/2 lb. ground beef
2 eggs
1 (14.5 oz.) can diced tomatoes with green chili peppers
1 tbsp onion powder

1 tbsp ground black pepper
1 tsp salt
1 slice white bread, cut into cubes
4 slices American cheese

## Directions

1. Set your oven to 350 degrees F before doing anything else.
2. In a large bowl, mix together the ground beef, eggs, diced tomatoes and green chili peppers, onion powder, ground black pepper, salt and bread.
3. Transfer the mixture into a 9x5-inch loaf pan and top with the cheese.
4. Cook in the oven for about for about 1 hour.

# *Tex Mex*
# Seafood Sampler

Prep Time: 15 min
Total Time: 40 min

Servings per Recipe: 6
| | |
|---|---|
| Calories | 528 kcal |
| Fat | 14.8 g |
| Carbohydrates | 50.6g |
| Protein | 46.3 g |
| Cholesterol | 232 mg |
| Sodium | 706 mg |

## Ingredients

1 (16 oz.) package uncooked wide egg noodles
1 tsp olive oil
1 lb. shark steaks, cut into chunks
1 lb. frozen medium shrimp

1 (14.5 oz.) can diced tomatoes and green chilis
2 C. shredded mozzarella cheese
ground black pepper to taste

## Directions

1. In a large pan of lightly salted boiling water, cook the egg noodles for about 6 – 8 minutes.
2. Drain well and keep aside.
3. In a bowl, mix together the shark, shrimp, tomatoes and green chilis.
4. In a skillet, heat the olive oil on medium heat and cook the shark mixture, covered for about 15 minutes.
5. Place the shark mixture over the cooked egg noodles and serve with a sprinkling of the mozzarella cheese and pepper.

# MEXICAN
# Mac n Cheese

 Prep Time: 10 mins

Total Time: 30 mins

Servings per Recipe: 6

| | |
|---|---|
| Calories | 384 kcal |
| Fat | 21.1 g |
| Carbohydrates | 27.1g |
| Protein | 19 g |
| Cholesterol | 73 mg |
| Sodium | 784 mg |

## Ingredients
1 lb. lean ground beef
1 (1.25 oz.) package taco seasoning mix
1 (7.3 oz.) package white Cheddar macaroni
and cheese mix
2 tbsp butter
1/4 C. milk

## Directions
1. Heat a large skillet on medium heat and cook the beef till browned completely.
2. Drain the excess grease from the skillet.
3. Add the taco seasoning and water according to seasoning package directions and simmer for about 10 minutes.
4. Remove from the heat and keep aside.
5. Prepare the macaroni and cheese according to package's directions, adding butter and milk as indicated.
6. Add the beef mixture and stir to combine.
7. Serve immediately.

# La Paz
# Corn Soup

Prep Time: 10 min
Total Time: 40 min

Servings per Recipe: 6
| | |
|---|---|
| Calories | 299 kcal |
| Fat | 18.6 g |
| Carbohydrates | 29.5g |
| Protein | 8.6 g |
| Cholesterol | 45 mg |
| Sodium | 706 mg |

## Ingredients

1 1/2 C. chopped onion
2 tbsp margarine
1 tbsp all-purpose flour
1 tbsp chili powder
1 tsp ground cumin
1 (16 oz.) package frozen corn kernels, thawed
2 C. medium salsa
1 (14.5 oz.) can chicken broth
8 oz. cream cheese, softened
1 C. milk

## Directions

1. In a large pan, melt the margarine and sauté the onion.
2. Stir in the flour, chili powder and cumin.
3. Add the corn, picante sauce and broth and bring to a boil.
4. Remove from the heat.
5. In a small bowl, add the cream cheese.
6. Gradually add 1/4 C. of the hot mixture into cream cheese and stir to combine well.
7. Add cream cheese mixture and milk into the pan, stirring till well combined and cook till heated completely.
8. Serve immediately.

La Paz Corn Soup

79

# FORT WORTH
# Party Dip

Prep Time: 15 mins
Total Time: 15 mins

Servings per Recipe: 6
| | |
|---|---|
| Calories | 299 kcal |
| Fat | 18.6 g |
| Carbohydrates | 29.5g |
| Protein | 8.6 g |
| Cholesterol | 45 mg |
| Sodium | 706 mg |

## Ingredients

1 (16 oz.) can refried beans
1 C. guacamole
1/4 C. mayonnaise
1 (8 oz.) container sour cream
1 (1 oz.) package taco seasoning mix
2 C. shredded Cheddar cheese

1 tomato, chopped
1/4 C. chopped green onions
1/4 C. black olives, drained

## Directions

1. In a large serving dish, spread the refried beans and top with the guacamole.

2. In a medium bowl, mix together the mayonnaise, sour cream and taco seasoning mix.

3. Spread the mayonnaise mixture over the layer of guacamole evenly, followed by a layer of the Cheddar cheese, tomato, green onions and black olives.

# Cajun Texas
# Sirloin Burgers

Prep Time: 25 min
Total Time: 40 min

Servings per Recipe: 4
Calories              714 kcal
Fat                   49.1 g
Carbohydrates         28.5g
Protein               38.3 g
Cholesterol           132 mg
Sodium                1140 mg

## Ingredients

1/2 C. mayonnaise
1 tsp Cajun seasoning
1 1/3 lb. ground beef sirloin
1 jalapeno pepper, seeded and chopped
1/2 C. diced white onion
1 clove garlic, minced
1 tbsp Cajun seasoning

1 tsp Worcestershire sauce
4 slices pepper jack cheese
4 hamburger buns, split
4 leaves lettuce
4 slices tomato

## Directions

1. Set your grill for medium-high heat and grease the grill grate.
2. In a small bowl, mix together the mayonnaise and 1 tsp of the Cajun seasoning.
3. In a large bowl, add the ground sirloin, jalapeño pepper, onion, garlic, 1 tbsp of the Cajun seasoning and Worcestershire sauce and mix till well combined.
4. Make 4 equal sized patties from the mixture.
5. Cook the patties on the grill for about 5 minutes from both sides.
6. During the last 2 minutes, place a cheese slice over each patty.
7. Spread the seasoned mayonnaise onto the insides of the buns evenly.
8. Arrange the burgers in the buns and top with the lettuce and tomato before serving.

# I HEART MEXICAN
# Chili

Prep Time: 15 mins
Total Time: 1 h 15 mins

Servings per Recipe: 4
Calories          657 kcal
Fat               18.3 g
Carbohydrates     82.4g
Protein           45.2 g
Cholesterol       87 mg
Sodium            541 mg

## Ingredients
1 1/2 C. dry black beans
2 tbsp olive oil
1 lb. ground turkey
1 large sweet onion, chopped
1 (28 oz.) can diced tomatoes
3 ears corn, kernels cut from cob
1 tbsp maple syrup
1 tbsp molasses
1 tbsp Hungarian paprika

1 tbsp chili powder
1 tbsp garlic powder
1/2 tsp chipotle chili powder
1/4 tsp cayenne pepper
sea salt to taste
1 (8 oz.) container plain yogurt (optional)
1 bunch green onions, diced (optional)

## Directions
1.  In a large pan, add the black beans and enough water to cover and bring to a boil.
2.  Reduce the heat to medium-low and simmer for about 30-40 minutes.
3.  Drain the beans and return into the pan.
4.  Meanwhile in a large cast-iron skillet, heat the olive oil on medium heat and stir fry the turkey for about 10 minutes.
5.  Add the sweet onion and cook, stirring for about 10 minutes.
6.  Add the turkey mixture into the pan with the black beans.
7.  Stir in the tomatoes, corn kernels, maple syrup, molasses, Hungarian paprika, chili powder, garlic powder, chipotle chili powder, cayenne pepper and sea salt and bring to a simmer.
8.  Cook for about 15-20 minutes.
9.  Serve with the topping of the yogurt and green onions.

# *Cinco De Mayo*
# Chili

🥣 Prep Time: 10 min

🕐 Total Time: 30 min

Servings per Recipe: 6

| | |
|---|---|
| Calories | 411 kcal |
| Fat | 17.2 g |
| Carbohydrates | 46.8g |
| Protein | 25.1 g |
| Cholesterol | 57 mg |
| Sodium | 1039 mg |

## Ingredients

1/4 C. Mazola(R) Corn Oil
1 lb. ground turkey
1 C. diced onion
1 tsp minced garlic
2 tbsp chili powder
1 tbsp ground cumin
1 tbsp chicken-flavored bouillon powder
1 (15 oz.) can black beans, rinsed and drained

1 (11 oz.) can Mexi-corn, drained
1 (12 oz.) package frozen diced butternut squash, thawed
1 (28 oz.) can crushed tomatoes
1 C. water
1/3 C. ketchup
Garnishes:
Shredded Mexican cheese, fresh cilantro, lime wedges, avocado slice

## Directions

1. In a large pan, heat the oil on medium heat and stir fry the turkey for about 5-7 minutes, breaking apart.
2. Add the onions, garlic, chili powder, cumin and bouillon powder and cook for about 3-5 minutes.
3. Stir in the vegetables, tomatoes, water and ketchup and bring to a boil.
4. Reduce the heat to low and simmer for about 10 minutes.
5. Serve with a topping of the desired garnishing.

# CLASSICAL
# Chicken Tacos

 Prep Time: 20 mins

Total Time: 1 h

Servings per Recipe: 12
| | |
|---|---|
| Calories | 403 kcal |
| Fat | 14.9 g |
| Carbohydrates | 49.3g |
| Protein | 18.8 g |
| Cholesterol | 39 mg |
| Sodium | 1049 mg |

## Ingredients
4 C. water
1 (16 oz.) package yellow rice
5 tbsp olive oil, divided (optional)
1 lb. boneless chicken, cut into 3/4-inch cubes
1 (1 oz.) package chicken taco seasoning mix
1 (16 oz.) can black beans, rinsed and drained

1 1/2 C. shredded Mexican cheese blend
1 (4 oz.) can sliced olives
1 jalapeno pepper, seeded and minced
12 corn tortillas
1 tbsp vegetable shortening

## Directions
1. In a pan, add the water and bring to a boil.
2. Add the rice and 1/4 C. of the olive oil and bring to a boil.
3. Reduce the heat to medium-low and simmer, covered for about 20-25 minutes.
4. In a skillet, heat 1 tbsp of the olive oil on medium heat and stir fry the chicken and taco seasoning mix for about 5-10 minutes.
5. Stir in the rice, black beans, Mexican cheese blend, olives, and jalapeño pepper and cook for about 5 minutes.
6. Heat another skillet on medium-high heat and warm each tortillas for about 1-2 minutes.
7. Fill each tortilla with about 1/2 C. of the chicken mixture, folding tortilla over filling.
8. In a skillet, heat the shortening on medium heat and fry the filled tortillas for about 2-3 minutes per side.

# Saturday Night
# Texan Rice

🥣 Prep Time: 10 min
🕐 Total Time: 40 min

Servings per Recipe: 6
Calories               177.0
Fat                    5.2g
Cholesterol            0.0mg
Sodium                 295.9mg
Carbohydrates          27.8g
Protein                4.1g

## Ingredients

2 cloves peeled and halved garlic
2 tbsp vegetable oil
1 C. long grain white rice ( not instant or fast cooking)

1 (14 1/2 oz.) cans chicken broth
1/4 C. salsa
1/4 C. chopped diced carrot
1/4 C. frozen corn

## Directions

1. In a heavy pan, heat the oil on high heat and cook the garlic till browned, stirring occasionally.
2. Remove the garlic cloves from the pan.
3. Add the rice into the garlic oil and reduce the heat to medium-high.
4. Cook, stirring constantly till the rice become brown.
5. Add broth, salsa, carrots and corn and reduce the heat to low.
6. Cook, covered for about 20 minutes.
7. With a fork, fluff the rice before serving.

# TRADITIONAL
# Mexican Spicy Vermicelli

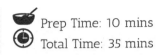

Prep Time: 10 mins
Total Time: 35 mins

Servings per Recipe: 4
| | |
|---|---|
| Calories | 311.6 |
| Fat | 7.9g |
| Cholesterol | 0.0mg |
| Sodium | 891.6mg |
| Carbohydrates | 51.7g |
| Protein | 9.2g |

## Ingredients

2 tbsp vegetable oil
1 medium onion, chopped
2 garlic cloves, minced
8 oz. vermicelli, broken up, 2 C.
1 tsp salt
1/2 tsp pepper

1/2 tsp cumin
1 (4 oz.) cans green chilies, chopped
1 (8 oz.) cans tomato sauce
2 C. water

## Directions

1. In a wide skillet, heat the oil on medium heat and cook the onion for about 10 minutes, stirring occasionally.
2. Add the garlic and cook for about 1-2 minutes.
3. Break the vermicelli into 2-inches pieces and add into the skillet.
4. Cook for about 3-4 minutes, stirring occasionally.
5. Add the salt, pepper, cumin, green chilies, tomato sauce and water and bring to a boil on high heat.
6. Reduce the heat to low and simmer, covered for about 10 minutes.

# A Tex-Mex Breakfast

🍳 Prep Time: 15 min

🕐 Total Time: 30 min

Servings per Recipe: 4
| | |
|---|---|
| Calories | 413.7 |
| Fat | 33.4g |
| Cholesterol | 230.5mg |
| Sodium | 945.7mg |
| Carbohydrates | 16.1g |
| Protein | 13.3g |

## Ingredients

3 C. Simply Potatoes® Shredded Hash Browns
1/2 tsp salt
2 tsp cumin, divided
1/2 tsp chili powder
1/2 C. panko breadcrumbs
1/3 C. Mexican cheese, shredded blend
3 tbsp vegetable oil

1 tbsp butter
4 eggs
2/3 C. sour cream
2 tbsp cilantro
2 tbsp sun-dried tomatoes, chopped
3 scallions, finely chopped
1/2 C. salsa
4 slices turkey bacon, cooked

## Directions

1. In a bowl, add the hash browns, salt, 1 tsp of the cumin, chili powder, panko and cheese and stir till well combined.
2. Divide the potato mixture into 4 portions.
3. In a large skillet, heat the oil on medium heat until hot and cook the potato stacks for about 3 minutes.
4. Carefully, flip the side and cook till golden from both sides.
5. Transfer the stacks into a dish and cover with a foil paper.
6. In a non-stick skillet, melt the butter on low heat.
7. Add the eggs, one at a time and cook for about 2-3 minutes.
8. Flip and cook till done completely.
9. Meanwhile in a small bowl, mix together the sour cream, cilantro, reserved cumin, tomatoes and the whites of the scallions.
10. Arrange 1 haystack on a small plate and top with an egg, followed by 2 tbsp of the salsa, a slice of bacon cut in half and crossed and a dollop of the sour cream.
11. Serve with a garnishing of the greens from the scallions.

# MEXICO CITY
# San Antonio Pierogies

 Prep Time: 30 mins

Total Time: 1 hr

Servings per Recipe: 6
| | |
|---|---|
| Calories | 561.4 |
| Fat | 33.3g |
| Cholesterol | 230.5mg |
| Sodium | 945.7mg |
| Carbohydrates | 16.1g |
| Protein | 13.3g |

## Ingredients
Dough
2 C. flour
1 egg, whisked
1/2 tsp salt
1/4 C. butter
1/2 C. sour cream
Filling
1 lb ground turkey
1/2 C. finely diced onion
2 minced garlic cloves
1/4 C. corn kernel (frozen)
3 chipotle peppers, minced
2 tbsp of the adobo sauce
1/4 tsp salt

1/2 tsp paprika
1/4 tsp cumin
1/4 tsp cayenne
1 C. chicken stock
2 C. Simply Potatoes Traditional Mashed
Potatoes
1/2 C. colby-monterey jack cheese
2 -3 tbsp melted butter
Dipping Sauce
1 C. sour cream
3 tbsp taco seasoning
1 tbsp chopped green onion

## Directions
1. For the dough in a food processor, pulse the flour and salt and pulse to break up any lumps.
2. Add the beaten egg and pulse 2-3 times.
3. Add the sour cream and butter and pulse for about 5-6 times.
4. Place the dough onto a smooth surface and shape into a ball.
5. In a plastic wrap, wrap the dough and refrigerate for at least 20 minutes.
6. For filling, heat a pan and cook the turkey till browned and then start breaking apart the meat.
7. Stir in the chopped onions, salt, paprika, cumin and cayenne and cook till the onions become softened.
8. Stir in the corn and chipotle peppers and garlic and cook for about 1 minute.
9. Stir in the Adobo Sauce and 1/4 C. of the chicken stock and cook, stirring till almost all the liquid is absorbed.
10. Add 1/4 C. of the chicken stock and cook, stirring till almost all the liquid is absorbed.

11. Now, add the remaining 1/2 C. of the chicken stock and cook, stirring till most of the liquid is absorbed.
12. Remove from the heat and keep aside to cool.
13. In a bowl, mix together the Simply Potatoes Mashed Potatoes and cheese.
14. Divide the dough into 1-inch balls and dust with the flour.
15. Place the dough onto a floured surface and roll into 3-4 inch rounds.
16. In the middle of each round, place a spoon full of the potato mixture, followed by a spoonful of the taco filling.
17. Fold in half and press together at the top.
18. Seal the edges tightly with wet fingers.
19. Arrange on a floured sheet pan.
20. In a pan of salted boiling water, cook 6-8 Pierogies at a time for about 8-10 minutes.
21. Remove from the pan and keep aside to cool slightly.
22. Coat with the melted butter on one side.
23. In a hot skillet, place the pierogies, buttered side down and cook till crisp.
24. Coat the tops with the butter and flip the side and cook till crisp.
25. For the dipping sauce in a bowl, mix together the sour cream, chopped green onion and taco seasoning.
26. Arrange the Pierogies on a platter with the dipping sauce and serve with a sprinkling of green onion.

# TEX MEX
# Pasta

Prep Time: 10 mins
Total Time: 20 mins

Servings per Recipe: 6
Calories          688.5
Fat               26.6g
Cholesterol       104.0mg
Sodium            850.0mg
Carbohydrates     75.8g
Protein           36.4g

## Ingredients

1 lb fusilli
3 tbsp butter
1/4 C. all-purpose flour
2 1/2 C. milk
1 tsp salt
2 C. old cheddar cheese, grated
2 C. diced cooked chicken

3/4 C. frozen corn
1/3 C. green onion, thinly sliced
1/3 C. salsa

## Directions

1. Prepare the pasta according to package's directions.
2. Drain and transfer into a large bowl.
3. Meanwhile, in a medium pan, melt the butter on medium heat and stir in the flour till blended.
4. Gradually add the milk and salt, beating continuously.
5. Bring to a boil, stirring continuously.
6. Reduce the heat to medium-low and simmer for about 1 minute.
7. Reduce the heat to low and slowly, add the cheese, stirring till melted.
8. Stir in the chicken, corn, green onions and salsa and cook till heated completely.
9. Transfer the chicken mixture into the bowl with the pasta and sprinkle with the additional grated Cheddar cheese if desired.

# *Santa Clara Bacon*
# Lettuce and Tomato

🥘 Prep Time: 10 min
🕐 Total Time: 15 min

Servings per Recipe: 2
| | |
|---|---|
| Calories | 2519.3 |
| Fat | 52.2g |
| Cholesterol | 58.0mg |
| Sodium | 5232.4mg |
| Carbohydrates | 387.1g |
| Protein | 127.3g |

## Ingredients

1/4 C. mayonnaise
1 pinch chili powder
1 pinch fresh jalapeno, chopped
1 pinch pepper
4 thick slices whole wheat bread
8 slices turkey bacon, crisply fried

6 slices tomatoes, thinly sliced
1 slice avocado, thinly sliced
1 sprig cilantro, roughly chopped
lettuce leaf, washed

## Directions

1. In a bowl, mix together the mayonnaise, pinch of chili powder and chopped fresh jalapeño pepper and keep aside.
2. Toast the bread slices lightly.
3. Spread the mayonnaise mixture over one side of each slice evenly.
4. Place the bacon over 2 slices, followed by the tomato, avocado, cilantro sprigs and lettuce.
5. Top with remaining 2 slice to make sandwiches.

# RIO RANCHO
# Deviled Eggs

 Prep Time: 30 mins
Total Time: 40 mins

Servings per Recipe: 6
Calories            135.9
Fat                 10.1g
Cholesterol         219.4mg
Sodium              364.3mg
Carbohydrates       3.1g
Protein             7.6g

## Ingredients
6 hard-boiled eggs, peeled
1 tbsp diced green onion
1 tbsp chopped fresh cilantro
1 small serrano peppers, seeded & finely chopped
1/4 C. mayonnaise

1 tsp prepared mustard
1/2 tsp salt
1/4 C. shredded cheddar cheese
chili powder

## Directions
1. Cut the eggs in half crosswise and carefully remove the yolks.
2. In a bowl, add the yolks and mash them.
3. Add the green onions, cilantro, Serrano peppers, mayonnaise, mustard and salt and stir to combine.
4. Place the egg yolk mixture into the egg whites and sprinkle with the cheese and chili powder.
5. Arrange the eggs in a dish and chill, covered before serving.

# Santa Fe
# Cheeseburgers

Prep Time: 5 min
Total Time: 20 min

Servings per Recipe: 4
| | |
|---|---|
| Calories | 354.3 |
| Fat | 21.5g |
| Cholesterol | 151.7mg |
| Sodium | 390.3mg |
| Carbohydrates | 6.1g |
| Protein | 32.3g |

## Ingredients

1 egg
1/4 C. well drained chunky salsa
1 tbsp Mexican seasoning

1 lb lean ground beef
1 C. shredded Monterey jack cheese
1/4 C. fine breadcrumbs

## Directions

1. Set your grill for medium heat and grease the grill grate.
2. In a medium bowl, add the egg and beat.
3. Add the salsa, seasoning, cheese, beef and bread crumbs and mix till well combined.
4. Make 4 equal sized patties.
5. Cook on the grill for about 15 minutes, flipping once in the middle way.

# HOUSTON
# Guacamole Sauce

Prep Time: 15 mins
Total Time: 1 hr 15 mins

Servings per Recipe: 15
Calories          178.5
Fat               16.5g
Cholesterol       20.2mg
Sodium            423.4mg
Carbohydrates     7.2g
Protein           2.7g

## Ingredients

4 medium avocados, peeled, pitted and cubed
1 (3 oz.) packages cream cheese, softened
1 (16 oz.) containers sour cream
1 (10 oz.) cans diced tomatoes with green chilies
1 tbsp garlic powder

2 tsp salt
1 tsp lemon juice
1 (4 oz.) cans diced green chilies (optional)
tortilla chips

## Directions

1. In a medium bowl add the avocados and cream cheese and mash to combine.
2. Add the remaining Ingredients except tortilla chips and mix till smooth.
3. Refrigerate, covered for at least 1 hour.
4. Serve with the tortilla chips for dipping.

# Tex Mex Vegan Lunch Box

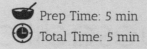 Prep Time: 5 min

Total Time: 5 min

Servings per Recipe: 4

| | |
|---|---|
| Calories | 208.9 |
| Fat | 2.8g |
| Cholesterol | 0.0mg |
| Sodium | 266.8mg |
| Carbohydrates | 36.9g |
| Protein | 9.7g |

## Ingredients

1 (15 oz.) cans black beans, rinsed and drained
2 tbsp lime juice
2 tbsp orange juice
2 cloves garlic, coarsely chopped
1/8 tsp salt

cayenne pepper
3 scallions, finely chopped
1/4 C. red bell peppers, finely chopped
4 flour tortillas
salsa

## Directions

1. In a food processor, add the beans, lime juice, orange juice, garlic, salt and cayenne pepper and pulse till smooth.
2. Transfer the mixture into a bowl and stir in the scallions and bell peppers.
3. Spread 1/4 of the mixture over each tortilla.
4. Roll the tortillas tightly and serve with a topping of the salsa.

# TEX MEX
# Quesadillas x Fajitas

Prep Time: 10 mins
Total Time: 25 mins

Servings per Recipe: 4
Calories             552 kcal
Fat                  31.1 g
Carbohydrates        40g
Protein              28 g
Cholesterol          79 mg
Sodium               859 mg

## Ingredients

2 tbsp vegetable oil, divided
1/2 onion, sliced
1/2 green bell pepper, sliced
salt to taste

4 flour tortillas
1/2 lb. cooked steak, cut into 1/4-inch thick pieces
1 C. shredded Mexican cheese blend

## Directions

1. In a 10-inch skillet, heat 2 tsp of the oil on medium heat and sauté the onion and green bell pepper for about 5-10 minutes.
2. Stir in the salt and transfer the mixture into a bowl.
3. Brush 1 side of each tortilla with the remaining oil.
4. In the same skillet, place 1 tortilla, oil-side down on medium heat.
5. Sprinkle with 1/2 of the steak, 1/2 of the onion mixture and 1/2 of the Mexican cheese mixture.
6. Place a second tortilla, oil-side up onto the cheese layer, pressing down with a spatula to seal.
7. Cook the quesadilla for about 3-4 minutes per side.
8. Remove the quesadilla from skillet and cut into wedges.
9. Repeat with the remaining ingredients for second quesadilla.

# Tex Mex
# Lasagna

Prep Time: 25 min
Total Time: 45 min

Servings per Recipe: 5
| | |
|---|---|
| Calories | 447 kcal |
| Fat | 24 g |
| Carbohydrates | 33.2g |
| Protein | 23.2 g |
| Cholesterol | 79 mg |
| Sodium | 899 mg |

## Ingredients

1 lb. lean ground beef
1 (1 oz.) package taco seasoning mix
1 (14 oz.) can peeled and diced tomatoes
with juice

10 (6 inch) corn tortillas
1 C. prepared salsa
1/2 C. shredded Colby cheese

## Directions

1. Set your oven to 350 degrees F before doing anything else.
2. Heat a large skillet on medium-high heat and cook the beef till browned completely.
3. Stir in the taco seasoning and tomatoes.
4. In the bottom of a 13x9-inch baking dish, arrange half of the tortillas evenly.
5. Place the beef mixture over the tortillas evenly.
6. Place the remaining tortillas over the beef mixture and top with the salsa, followed by the cheese.
7. Cook in the oven for about 20-30 minutes.

# BAKED BEAN BURRITOS
# Texas Mexican Style

Prep Time: 15 mins
Total Time: 25 mins

Servings per Recipe: 8
Calories                275.9
Fat                     7.4g
Cholesterol             10.5mg
Sodium                  756.4mg
Carbohydrates           41.1g
Protein                 12.4g

## Ingredients
1 (14 oz.) cans vegetarian baked beans, in tomato sauce
1/2 tbsp chili powder
1/2 tsp oregano
1/2 tsp cumin
64 inches flour tortillas
1/2 C. part-skim mozzarella cheese, shredded
1/2 C. low-fat cheddar cheese, shredded
1/2 C. salsa
1/2 C. pepper, chopped (optional)
1/4 C. nonfat sour cream (optional)

## Directions
1. In a food processor, add the beans and seasonings and pulse till smooth.
2. Spread 8 tortillas onto smooth surface.
3. Place the bean mixture in the center of each tortilla evenly.
4. Sprinkle with mozzarella and cheddar cheese, followed by the salsa, chopped pepper and sour cream.
5. Fold the tortillas up into burritos.
6. Place burritos in a nonstick frying pan on medium heat and cook till golden brown.

# November's
# Spicy Salsa

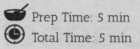 Prep Time: 5 min
Total Time: 5 min

| Servings per Recipe: 1 jar | |
| --- | --- |
| Calories | 356.3 |
| Fat | 0.6g |
| Cholesterol | 0.0mg |
| Sodium | 70.0mg |
| Carbohydrates | 90.9g |
| Protein | 1.0g |

## Ingredients

1 (16 oz.) cans whole berry cranberry sauce

1/4 C. canned jalapeno, chopped

1 green onions or 1 scallion, sliced

1 tsp dried cilantro

1 tsp ground cumin

1 tsp lime juice

## Directions

1. In a medium bowl, mix together all the Ingredients.
2. Refrigerate for up to 1 week.

# SAN ANTONIO
# Stroganoff

 Prep Time: 10 mins

Total Time: 30 mins

Servings per Recipe: 6
| | |
|---|---|
| Calories | 499.4 |
| Fat | 15.4g |
| Cholesterol | 138.9mg |
| Sodium | 691.4mg |
| Carbohydrates | 54.9g |
| Protein | 35.6g |

## Ingredients

12 oz. extra wide egg noodles
1 tbsp butter, tossed with cooked noodles
1 1/2 lbs extra lean ground beef
1/2 C. chopped onion
3 (10 oz.) cans rotel, the diced tomatoes
with green chilies (undrained)
1 C. frozen corn, thawed
1/4 C. water
1 tsp ground cumin

1/2 tsp garlic powder
1/4-1/2 tsp cayenne pepper
1/2 tsp pepper
salt, to taste
1 C. reduced-fat sour cream
1/4 C. chopped fresh cilantro, for garnish

## Directions

1. In large pan of the boiling water, prepare the egg noodles according to the package's directions.
2. Drain well and return to the pan and toss with the butter.
3. Cover the pan to keep.
4. Meanwhile, heat a large skillet on medium heat and cook the beef and onion till browned completely.
5. Drain the excess grease from the skillet.
6. Add the Rotel, corn, water, cumin, garlic powder, cayenne, pepper and salt and bring to a gentle simmer.
7. Cook for about 10 minutes.
8. Stir in the reduced-fat sour cream and stir to blend well.
9. Cook till heated completely.
10. Serve over the hot cooked noodles with a garnishing of the chopped cilantro.

# Mexican
# Potatoes

Prep Time: 5 min
Total Time: 5 min

Servings per Recipe: 1 tray
| | |
|---|---|
| Calories | 112.3 |
| Fat | 4.1g |
| Cholesterol | 9.0mg |
| Sodium | 260.3mg |
| Carbohydrates | 15.5g |
| Protein | 3.7g |

## Ingredients

8 medium baking potatoes, baked and cooled slightly
6 oz. Italian turkey sausage
2/3 C. salsa
1 C. nacho cheese sauce

sour cream (optional)
sliced green onion (optional)
sliced ripe olives (optional)

## Directions

1. Set your oven to 425 degrees F before doing anything else.
2. Cut the baked potatoes in half lengthwise and scoop out the flesh, leaving about 1/4-inch shell.
3. Arrange the potato shells onto an ungreased baking sheet.
4. Heat a large skillet and cook the sausage till browned completely.
5. Drain the excess grease from the skillet.
6. Stir in the salsa and cook for about 2 minutes.
7. Place the sausage mixture into the potato shells and top with the nacho cheese sauce.
8. Cook in the oven for about 10-15 minutes.
9. Serve with a topping of a sour cream, some green onions and a few ripe olives.

# MEXICAN
# Chowder

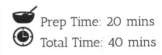 Prep Time: 20 mins
Total Time: 40 mins

Servings per Recipe: 16
Calories            187.9
Fat                 6.8g
Cholesterol         42.7mg
Sodium              725.6mg
Carbohydrates       16.4g
Protein             15.2g

## Ingredients
1 large onion, chopped
1 C. thinly sliced celery
2 cloves garlic, minced
1 tbsp oil
1 1/2 lbs boneless skinless chicken breast
halves, cut into bite size pieces
2 (14 1/2 oz.) cans chicken broth
1 (32 oz.) packages frozen hash brown
potatoes ( loose-pack diced)
1 (2 2/3 oz.) packages country gravy mix

2 C. milk
1 (8 oz.) packages processed cheese spread,
cut into chunks ( such as Velveeta)
1 (16 oz.) jars chunky salsa
1 (4 1/2 oz.) cans diced green chilies
corn chips

## Directions
1. In a large Dutch oven, heat the oil on medium heat and sauté the onion, celery and garlic for about 5 minutes.
2. Add the chicken and cook and stir fry for about 2-3 minutes.
3. Add the broth and potatoes and bring to a boil.
4. Reduce the heat and simmer, covered for about 12-15 minutes, stirring occasionally.
5. In a medium bowl, add the gravy mix and milk and stir to combine.
6. Stir the milk mixture into the soup mixture.
7. Stir in the cheese, salsa and green chilies and reduce the heat to low.
8. Cook and stir till the cheese is melted completely.
9. Serve with the corn chips.

Made in United States
Cleveland, OH
08 March 2025

15004373R00057